# Coaching Questions for Every Situation

*A Leader's Guide to Asking Powerful Questions for Breakthrough Results*

Jeremy Kourdi

NICHOLAS BREALEY
PUBLISHING

London • Boston

First published by Nicholas Brealey Publishing in 2021
An imprint of John Murray Press
A division of Hodder & Stoughton Ltd,
An Hachette UK company

1

A CIP catalogue record for this title is available from the British Library

Trade Paperback ISBN 9781529349832
eBook ISBN UK 9781529349856 / US 9781529355819

Typeset by KnowledgeWorks Global Ltd.

Printed and bound in Great Britain by Clays Ltd, Elcograf S.p.A.

John Murray Press policy is to use papers that are natural, renewable
and recyclable products and made from wood grown in sustainable
forests. The logging and manufacturing processes are expected to
conform to the environmental regulations of the country of origin.

John Murray Press                    Nicholas Brealey Publishing
Carmelite House                        Hachette Book Group
50 Victoria Embankment      Market Place, Center 53, State Street
London EC4Y 0DZ                   Boston, MA 02109, USA

www.nicholasbrealey.com

To my colleagues and everyone I have ever coached – thank you for your openness, insight and diligence, and very best wishes for the future.

# Contents

# Contents

# The Guiding Principles and Techniques of Coaching

Why do we ask questions?

The answer to this question – the first of the many hundreds of questions in this book – is interesting and surprising, and varies widely depending on who is asking the question, who and what exactly is being asked as well as how and when. The truth is that we ask questions for many, many reasons, and not simply to get an answer. For example, we ask questions so that we can hold someone to account for their actions (Why did you do that? Did you know you were breaking the rules?). So that we can develop confidence or reassurance (Is that the best option? Are we – am I – doing the right thing? How will we know if we succeed?). So that we can show empathy and support (Are you OK? How can I help?). So we can deepen our understanding (Why?). So we can challenge authority (Why not?). Or possibly, to increase engagement or to deepen our pool of expertise (What do you think?). Questions work to help us succeed in business (What do our customers want? How is the market changing?), or to plan and prepare (When? Who?). The list goes on.

Great questions provide answers and generate understanding, of course, but they provide so much more. In a business context characterized by deep uncertainty, breath-taking challenges, opportunity and change, a blurring of traditional boundaries between work and home life, and a deep desire to survive and thrive, questions are the way we make progress. We do this not only by increasing understanding but also by building confidence in ourselves and others, developing our mindset, shifting our behaviour, preparing and rehearsing, reflecting and, perhaps most of all, learning. In a coaching context these are some of the biggest benefits and reasons why we pose questions.

This highlights two sometimes neglected points about questions: the importance of *context* and *motives* (closely linked to mindset). What matters when questioning is not simply what is said, but how, when and why it is said as well. It is important not to confuse genuine questions with emotional outbursts, passive aggression or other behaviours. 'Why don't you just leave?' may be a genuine question in some instances – for example, to a victim of abuse – while at other times it may be statement of emotion – possibly passive aggression.

## Questioning – an essential leadership skill

Coaching and questioning are essential and complementary leadership skills: they are essential tools in professional coaching situations, where the skill of a coach is often to be non-directive and goal-oriented, and to help someone find the best way forward for them. Questioning is also an essential leadership skill, vital for setting direction and mobilizing and engaging people.

For experienced coaches questioning is a vital, indispensable tool – one that enables them to quickly show their interest, provide a feeling of support and build rapport. It also enables the coach to uncover and explore issues and truths and help the individual they are working with to better understand goals, options, realities, ideas and potential changes. Above all, perhaps, great questioning helps people to think about issues in a different, more constructive, insightful and valuable way.

## The guiding principles behind coaching questions

### 1 A positive mindset is essential

Mindset matters, and that mindset needs to be full of positive intent. Leading questions – and questions which include some degree of 'manipulation' that is not in the coachee's best interest – are to be avoided.

## 2 A growth mindset is invaluable

Coaches and coachees both benefit from a growth mindset, particularly as it enables them to learn about fields that are outside their area of expertise. They make new and interesting connections and are progress-oriented in their style and approach. Individuals who believe their talents can be developed have a growth mindset, and they are more likely to have the adaptability, drive and progressive view needed to connect with others, deliver results and succeed. This contrasts with individuals who believe they are innately gifted and talented, and so possess a fixed mindset. People with a growth mindset are keen to learn about fields that are outside their area of expertise, and are therefore more able to make new and interesting connections and be creative in their problem-solving.

## 3 When questioned, people may reasonably need time to respond

Don't rush, interrupt or feel that you need to fill the silence – let people have time to reflect and frame their response.

## 4 Usually the best question is the one that is simplest and most obvious

Don't try to be too clever! If someone seems upset, or shows any distinct emotion, then explore it with them. What happened? Why do they feel this way? What, if anything, needs to be done as a result? What can we learn? What are the implications? Where do we go from here? How can I help? What do you need?

## 5 Use questions to hold up a mirror to the coachee, in particular by focusing on the language that is being used

I once coached someone who told me that their priority was to '… smash the opposition, just bury them. We need to leave our competitors trailing in the dust while we power ahead. To do this we need to marshal all of our resources – all of them, especially our people – and make sure our work has a laser-like focus.' The coachee said this all very seriously and with a powerful intensity and energy that were almost palpable. Later in the conversation they seemed surprised when part of their 360-degree feedback made reference to their aggressive approach. 'Can you see why people might think that?' I asked. 'No! I'm a pussycat!' was the indignant reply. 'OK,' I said soothingly. 'Well...' I then shared what I had experienced earlier with their language and explored the issue with the coachee. While not necessarily a negative attribute in some circumstances, was it their intention to come across as aggressive? How intentional was their use of language? What about empathy...? And so the conversation developed in a way that helped them develop greater self-awareness, understand the feedback they had received, and modulate their approach.

## 6 Ask helpful questions, and be bold if necessary

When asking a question that seeks to get to the complicated heart of a difficult or personal issue, it can be tempting to sidestep issues.

## 7 Be sensitive: sometimes questions are inappropriate and wrong

Questioning is one of the most valuable, meaningful skills that anyone can possess – together with empathy. Crucially, the two should work together.

## 8 Use questions to provide support and challenge

The essence of coaching is to give the person you are coaching both support and challenge, so you should recognize that explicitly and ensure that questions keep this in mind. In particular, don't be afraid of using questions to *challenge*. 'Why did you feel that was the best approach?' is a challenging question. There may be a valuable, revealing answer, or there may not, but crucially it pushes and explores. Ultimately however, questioning needs to be accompanied with genuine interest, a reason for asking (and providing support and challenge) and positive intent as well.

## 9 How you question is important, not simply what you say

When you ask something, the context, body language and tone all make a significant difference. If your approach and mindset are in the right place, then this will follow, but make sure that you are in a positive place when questioning.

## 10 Be intentional: balance art and science; emotion and intellect

Questioning is not always easy for everyone. Some people refer constantly to pre-prepared notes; others prefer to be more organic, operating 'on the fly'. Experience suggests that the best approach – the one that is suitable in most instances – is a balance of art and science, emotion and intellect. Be objective in your analysis of the questions to ask and the responses you receive, but show empathy, humanity and – when appropriate – emotion (surprise, curiosity, kindness and many others) as well.

## 11 Remember that questions take you down a path, especially when the questions (and the path) are significant

Sometimes, when asking questions, people can jump around too much, rather than staying the course and fully exploring the issue. So, for example, if you ask someone to give you an overview of their career and they say, 'And then I lost my job', your next question should really not be, 'OK – so, what's in your in tray at the moment?' It is almost always best if the next question relates to the significant fact they have just shared. In other words, keep with the subject, especially if it's significant. For example, if someone tells you they lost their job, useful questions to ask would be, 'How did you feel?', 'What did you do?' or 'What did you learn?'

## 12 Focus on the person in front of you

Newsflash: some people (I would argue a majority of people, worldwide) like talking about themselves! That's fine if the talky person is the one you are coaching, but it's not brilliant if it applies to you *when you coach*. So, focus on the other person deeply, genuinely, and with honesty and openness. The single-most effective way to do this is with questions that show interest, establish rapport, set the tone, and, most obviously, encourage the coachee to open up.

### 13 Be authentic – find your own personal questioning style

Don't ask something that feels unnatural or wrong. Great questions emerge from who we are and how we think, and while we can hear and borrow great questions from other coaches, we need to frame them and use them in the way that is most effective and genuine for us as individuals. Closely linked is the fact that the ability to ask great questions emerges over time; this is entirely appropriate, of course, as the greatest value of coaching questions lies in their ability to develop and improve our thinking. In this way, not only does the coachee benefit from great questions, the coach does as well.

Before we move on to the questions that form the heart of this book, let's first look at some of the essential principles and techniques that underpin all coaching questions.

## What is coaching?

There are many different types of coaching – for example, sports coaching, life coaching, directive and non-directive coaching – as well as different expectations of what coaching can achieve.

Coaching is goal-oriented, non-directive and learner-led, with the coach helping an individual develop their thinking or skills, successfully resolve an issue or challenge, or achieve or progress a goal. Crucially, coaching is more to do with *attitude* than skills. In the words of the coaching pioneer and writer Sir John Whitmore, coaching is about 'unlocking an individual's potential to maximize their own performance'. Achieving this requires the coach to provide both support and challenge. That is the essence of great coaching. In this book, it is assumed that most coaching will take place in the context of an organization, with a coach working with a leader or manager.

Coaching relies on several fundamental, related skills as well as active listening and questioning. These skills include:

- giving and receiving feedback (positive, non-judgemental feedback in particular)

- demonstrating a positive regard and intent, and seeking to help the person being coached

- being objective in your analysis of the person being coached and the issue being discussed

- evaluating what to do and when to help the person develop, learn and grow

- consistently maintaining high standards of professionalism and integrity at all times

- establishing rapport and displaying skills of assertion – in particular, being warm and supportive while also challenging the person being coached.

This means that effective coaches trust and accept learners for who they are as individuals; they provide encouragement and support, especially after setbacks and mistakes; and they give specific praise – in fact, they offer more praise than criticism in respect of mistakes.

Coaches also set an example and demonstrate effective behaviours, and they are competent, respected and able to deliver on their commitments. In addition, they avoid using their authority or power, preferring instead to communicate well and often, remaining in touch and helping to keep people informed. They set positive expectations, respect confidentiality, and, crucially, they help the person being coached find the answer for themselves. In this way, they build confidence as well as developing experience and shaping mindsets.

**What great coaches do:**

- Keep an open mind and positive approach

- Listen and question

- View coaching as a relationship of equals

- Have a structure

- Believe the person is resourceful and can be even better

- Help the person clarify their issue and be specific about what needs to change

- Remember it is about helping the person to be more effective

- Give lots of positive, genuine and specific feedback

- Put the discussion in the context of the person being coached

- Work with the person's own experience

- Keep in mind the focus and goals of the person

- Maintain rapport and develop the relationship

- Work with the reality of the person and respond to them and their issues

**And what coaches avoid:**

- Prejudging

√ - Giving advice

√ - Playing the expert

✓ • Adhering too rigidly to a structure or coaching process

✓ • Believing it's about the coach fixing the coachee

- Making assumptions or leaving things woolly

- Making the coachee comfortable at the expense of effectiveness

- Giving any negative feedback unless it is a practical idea for improvement

- Putting it in the coach's own context at the expense of the coachee's

- Failing to share their own experience if it would help the person being coached

- Forgetting that the coach-coachee relationship is important and that the coachee is human

✓ • Becoming a counsellor, mentor or someone the person is dependent upon

### Checklist: succeeding as a coach

Great coaches possess the following capabilities and skills, and because they are coaches they constantly work at developing and furthering these skills.

Great coaches...

- ... are always 'present' and recognize that their behaviour sets the tone. For example, it is tempting to view rapport building as the preamble to a coaching session. This is wrong: it *is* the coaching session. Rapport combined with a focus on the individual leads to greater trust, openness and understanding. Without rapport, it will be harder to achieve focus or generate personal, practical insight – and the results of coaching will be limited at best. Rapport is there when we feel we have nothing to fear from the other person and they feel the same about us. This is especially significant with coaching where sensitive personal issues come to the fore.

- **... agree the framework for the coaching sessions.** They confirm the time available and any other arrangements, including confidentiality. It is vital not to be casual about the 'formal' aspects of coaching – they are essential.

- **... don't avoid discussing spirituality or personal issues.** If you want to coach and focus on personal development, then you need to recognize all of the influences affecting a person's goals, reality, options and will – especially their personal views and values. During coaching sessions the coachee often describes a relevant issue from their personal life that affects their 'business' issue.

- **... are patient and thoroughly explore all the issues.** It takes time to get to the heart of a coachee's issue, and for a busy executive or an impatient coach this can be perilous, notably because:
  - it can lead to truncated or weak questioning and flawed assumptions
  - it results in interruptions and distractions
  - it can lead to misdirected thinking and a focus on the peripheral issues.

The priority is to stay focused on the coachee's issues and diligently explore their situation. Look for what they are not saying, as well as what they are, and take notice of body language and tone.

- **... are generous, supportive and positive – helping people to work at their best.** Coaching relies on empathy combined with a clear-eyed, objective approach. Clearly, the coach needs to be completely on the coachee's side, helping them succeed with their issues. However, it is important not to get involved personally in the coachee's issue.

- **... pay attention to the process!** When you are coaching someone it is vital to pay attention to what the individual is saying and how they are saying it.
  - Note the presenting issue – what seems to be the issue that the individual wants to address?
  - Is it a simple behavioural process in which you have to show or do something that they can model?
  - Is this about giving the individual more skills and further training? Is this what they are asking for?
  - Why is this issue important? How is it being articulated: are you being asked for guidance or reasons; is this about how the person feels they are being treated or not treated; or is this about fairness or respect?
  - Is this a personal issue in which the person wants to be acknowledged personally in some way?
  - Is this about their role and how they perceive themselves and how others will perceive them?
  - Is this role a statement about them at a personal level, and do they feel that their status will be, or is being, affected?

- **... introduce different models and techniques.** They make sure that the right technique is introduced appropriately, in the right way and at the right time.

- **... recognize that people bring their own issues, experiences and personality to every coaching issue.** When coaching someone, remember that, if they say or think something, then that is their reality. Simply contradicting them will rarely change what a person thinks or feels. A better approach – perhaps the only effective place to start – is to talk to the person about what they think or feel, and why.

## Understand the different types of coaching question, and develop your own style

In the context of coaching, questioning is the route to progress. This is because questions enable the people being coached to arrive at their own solutions and, crucially, to 'own' them as well. The effectiveness of this tool applies to anyone in a coaching role, whether as a leader, a professional coach, or a people management executive.

However, despite the significance and value of coaching questions, there is limited understanding of:

- **context-specific questions** – specifically, what to ask in typical and difficult situations.

- **the guiding principles behind great questions** – how to think like a great questioner, the rules of questioning, the pitfalls to avoid and the essential skills behind great questions.

This book addresses this need and provides a practical guide to asking great questions.

It is vital that you are comfortable asking questions and exploring issues in the best way for the coachee *and yourself*. Even so, there are several fundamental – almost universal – questions that can help at any time, and are especially valuable as a 'go to' place when things get tough. These include:

- What is your ideal?

- What is your goal?

- What are your options?

- What is the best (or least worst) option?

- What is stopping you?

- What can you do about that?

- Why do you think that? How do you feel about that?

## The questions every coach needs to have ready: the GROW model

The GROW model, developed by Sir John Whitmore, provides a framework for coaching. GROW is an acronym with four stages: Goals, Reality, Options and Way forward (also Will/When).

With the GROW model, responsibility for setting goals, understanding reality, generating options and taking action rests with the coachee. The coach's role is to help by facilitating this process, helping the coachee to focus, encouraging them to develop a comprehensive and insightful perspective, and testing their approach.

The GROW model is usually, but not necessarily, a linear process, meaning you can move up and down between stages. The key points are that the process is goal-oriented, learner-led and leading to an outcome – the achievement of that goal.

### Goals

This stage focuses on the coachee's goals – their aims and priorities. It sets the agenda for the coaching conversation. During this stage the coach should be flexible and prepared to explore, question and challenge. This is achieved with questioning and empathy. The outcome of this stage is a clear set of goals both for the overall coaching relationship and, in particular, for that coaching session. Questions include:

- What is your goal? What are your priorities? What are you trying to achieve?

- How will you know when you have achieved it?

- Is the goal SMART – specific, motivating, attainable, relevant and trackable?

- How will you know when it has been achieved? What will success look like?

## Reality

The next step is exploring the coachee's current position – their reality and concerns relating to their specific goal. The coach needs to help the coachee quickly analyse the most significant issues relating to their goal. The coach can also help by providing information and by summarizing the situation. Questions include:

- To what extent can you control the result? What sort of things can't you control?

- When do you want to achieve the goal by? How feasible is this?

- What are the milestones or key points on the way to achieving your goal?

- Who is involved and what effect could they have on the situation?

- What have you done about this situation so far, and what have been the results?

- What are the major constraints or issues you are (or will be) encountering?

- What other issues are occurring at work that might have a bearing on your goal?

## Options

During this stage of the process the coach helps the coachee to generate options, strategies and action plans for achieving their goal. Questions include:

- What options do you have?

- Which options do you favour and why?

- If you had unlimited resources, what options would you have?

- Could you link your goal to some other issue?

- What would be the perfect solution?

### Way forward (also Will/When)

The final stage is vital, yet it is often neglected or rushed. The aim is to clearly agree what needs to be done; what action will be taken, by whom, how and when, and to ensure that sufficient commitment is present to see this through. Typically, the coach's role is to provide a sounding board, highlighting strengths and weaknesses, testing the approach and offering an additional perspective that supports the coachee. Questions at this stage include:

What are you going to do?
When are you going to do it?
Who needs to know?
What support and resources do you need, and how will you get them?
What obstacles might you face? How will you ensure success?

## Questions to ask when setting goals

A starting point frequently used in coaching, notably by managers who are coaches, is goal setting. Given its significance and popularity, this issue is explored in detail in Chapter 2. However, because goal setting is also important as a foundation for all great questioning, it is briefly included here as well.

Goals are often SMART: specific; motivating (or measurable); attainable; relevant; trackable (or timely, or time-constrained). When goal setting, it can help to focus your own and your coachee's thinking on the following issues and questions:

| Coaching issues and priorities | Questions to help the coachee |
| --- | --- |
| *Specific*<br>Goals need to be granular, practical and easy to implement and progress, so: what exactly is the goal or task, and why is it significant? | What does a good job or successful outcome look like?<br>When does the goal or task need to be accomplished?<br>How will you approach the challenge?<br>What resources or support do you need? |
| *Motivating*<br>The best goals are appealing and motivational, so: is the goal or task meaningful for the individual? | Will working on this goal build competence and commitment?<br>Why does this goal matter to you? Is it sufficiently motivating?<br>Will working on this goal add or drain energy?<br>How will you sustain energy and commitment? |
| *Attainable*<br>There's no room for confusion: customers and colleagues need you to deliver when expected. So: can you achieve this goal within the required timescale? | Is the goal attainable with current resources and workload?<br>Is the goal realistic, reasonable and achievable?<br>Is the goal entirely within your control? If not, what will you do to ensure it is achieved? |
| *Relevant*<br>Relevance and ruthless prioritization are crucial and closely connected, and what matters is doing the activities and achieving the goals of highest value. For this reason you need to be sure that the goal clearly aligns with your team's objectives. Can you describe the link, and is the goal sufficiently relevant? | What makes the goal or task significant and valuable for the organization?<br>Is the goal or task aligned with organization and work team goals?<br>Is the goal or task a high priority in relation to other goals? |

| Coaching issues and priorities | Questions to help the coachee |
|---|---|
| *Trackable*<br>Goals need to be trackable and measurable. How will you measure and track progress towards achieving this goal? | What is the vision – the ideal outcome?<br>What is the plan – how will you achieve the goal, and how will you start?<br>What are the key milestones?<br>How will you measure progress and success? |

## What would a coach say to you? Mastering the art of self-coaching

The same questioning approach used by the coach or mentor can also be used for self-coaching; all you need to do is consider a major issue at work that you would like to resolve. This is a useful technique and helpful as a way of developing a coaching mindset. It is a useful muscle to exercise! So, when appropriate, try asking yourself:

- What are you trying to achieve?

- How will you know when you have achieved it?

- Would you define it as an end goal or a performance goal?

- If it is an end goal, what performance goal could be related to it?

- Is the goal specific and measurable?

- To what extent can you control the result? What sort of things won't you have control over?

- Do you feel that achieving the goal will stretch or break you?

- When do you want to achieve the goal by?

- What are the milestones or key points on the way to achieving your goal?

- Who is involved, and what effect could they have on the situation?

- What have you done about this situation so far, and what have been the results?

- What are the major constraints in finding a way forward?

- Are these constraints major or minor? How could their effect be reduced?

- What other issues are occurring at work that might have a bearing on your goal?

- What options do you have?

- If you had unlimited resources, what options would you have?

- Could you link your goal to some other organizational issue?

- What would be the perfect solution?

The essence of great coaching is, of course, a mindset that is full of positive intent, open and curious. When you are coaching, therefore, the questions to ask yourself include: what is the best way to support this person? What is their goal? How do they feel at the moment?

## How this book is organized

Each chapter begins with a short overview of the subject and its context, as well as one or more useful techniques or issues to keep in mind, before moving on to present the questions that are typically most effective.

The book is divided into three parts:

**Part 1 explores** *personal coaching questions.* The chapters in this section are designed to help with some of the most common and toughest coaching issues of all – those relating to an individual's personal effectiveness, behaviour, mindset, their understanding of themselves and, ultimately, their sense of fulfilment. Chapters successively explore an individual's personal style and approach, their emotional intelligence, emotions and resilience, readiness to learn and adapt, their ability to shift behaviour and mindset (these are among the toughest questions), the way they make decisions and solve problems, and their purpose.

**Part 2 focuses on** *typical and difficult coaching challenges.* These are the issues that organizations most often look to coaches to help with, and which individuals commonly share with their coach as being the topics where they would value greatest support. Issues here include developing leadership, teamwork, coaching across cultures, helping a colleague who is disengaged, supporting someone through a period of uncertainty, crisis, disruption, challenge or change and, finally, helping to develop communication and influencing skills.

**Part 3 is concerned with** *defining moments of leadership* – situational coaching questions focusing on those times where individuals especially value coaching. These include starting in a new role, seeking feedback, reviewing a project or event and planning for the future.

The starting point with great coaching, as always, is the individual, and so it is with *personal coaching questions* that we will begin.

# PART 1

# Personal Coaching Questions

The chapters in this part of the book focus on the personal issues that shape an individual's effectiveness and mindset. These issues include the self-awareness, emotional intelligence, relationship building skills, energy and resilience, and the ability to learn and adapt, handle tough challenges, make the best decisions and choices, solve problems, and chart the right course that will drive an individual towards greater personal fulfilment and success.

While these questions are intended to be used by the coach/leader who is coaching a client or colleague, they are also hugely effective for self-coaching. In other words, coaches can usefully reflect on many of these questions themselves.

This highlights a significant point about coaching: while many of the issues discussed during a coaching conversation are extrinsic – meaning that they relate to external factors such as decisions or events – the place to start is actually the individual's mindset. In other words, it helps to know what to expect and to prepare for it, and that applies both to the coach and the coachee.

# CHAPTER 1

## Questions about You

Self-awareness is a vital attribute when coaching, learning, leading or doing pretty much anything. It is vital in questioning for several fundamental reasons:

1. It helps build understanding about:
   - how your questions and your approach are being received generally
   - the progress, or otherwise, that you are making
   - the impact you are having.

2. It ensures that you are able to play to your strengths and minimize the effect of your weaknesses. Crucially, self-awareness is an important way marker on the road to humility, self-improvement, understanding, empathy and progress. The alternatives to being self-aware are not good! Antonyms include clueless, uninformed, oblivious.

3. The ability to elevate personal performance and lead with impact starts with each of us personally. After all, we can't expect someone to do something that we either do not fully understand, or that we do not value for ourselves.

4. We need to be seen to develop our own performance. This is vital not only for your own personal effectiveness but also because:
   - it drives and encourages your coachees to improve
   - it enables us to ensure our skills and mindset remain current, relevant and agile
   - it is how we shape a culture of performance.

## How can I develop greater self-awareness in myself and others?

Four simple methods can help develop self-awareness and an understanding of our impact on others:

1. **Ask for feedback.** Do this often and routinely, and from a wide range of people at all levels in the business and across all aspects of your life.

2. **Work with a coaching supervisor.** Supervision is essential for professional coaching. Essentially, it is a form of coaching for coaches, but much more specifically focused on:
   • how the coach feels, and why
   • troubleshooting any issues or concerns
   • providing a sounding board or 'sense check' for the coaches' responses
   • maintaining self-awareness and understanding any development needs.

3. **Rigorously develop personal insight.** This may take the form of a psychometric assessment test or 360-degree feedback. Choose whatever suits your context and preference. It may only need to happen occasionally, but it needs to happen. A good starting point is to look at yourself and identify your:
   • Weaknesses
   • Strengths
   • Limits
   • Motivations
   • Personal and professional goals
   • Needs
   • Values
   • Priorities
   • Dominant emotions.

You will then start to build up a picture of how others see and experience you because all of these factors influence how you behave. At that point, you can ask yourself whether that is how you would like to be experienced, and if it's not, you can begin to think about what you might need to change.

## 4. Use the Leader's Shadow (see box).

### The Leader's Shadow

The Leader's Shadow is a way to develop self-awareness, enabling individuals to focus on their impact on others – a vital issue when coaching. The Leader's Shadow also enables leaders and coaches to understand and embrace their personal style, become aware of areas of strength and weakness, and recognize their sphere of influence and impact.

To use the technique, first think about each element and then write down the following in each quadrant:

- **What I say** – how I set context and frame issues, the key messages I convey and what I repeat or emphasize
- **How I act** – my behaviours, symbols, relationships
- **What I measure** – the things I look at and take an interest in, where I focus, what I reward and where I give recognition
- **What I prioritize** – whether disciplines or routines, along with the people I interact with

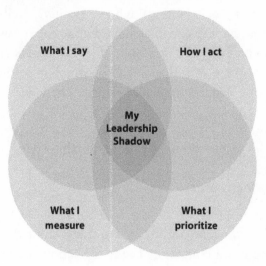

The Leader's Shadow

Next, review each quadrant: where are there contradictions? For example, do you say it is important to be open and approachable, and then sit in closed-door meetings or work without communicating? What should you enhance, emphasize or adjust in order to increase your congruence as a leader?

After completing the framework, share your reflections with a coach.

## What does 'good' look like?

Self-aware people are typically *at ease with themselves*; secure in what they know and what they do not. This security enables them to be *open, curious and other-oriented*.

When coaching, it is valuable to be able to *connect* with people, establishing understanding and making clear your positive intent, and also to *challenge* them positively and constructively. These two behaviours – connection and challenge – are mutually reinforcing. Connection matters because it gives us permission to challenge (e.g. by questioning), while a positive, well-intentioned challenge is valuable because it can be a vital way for us to improve and develop an even stronger bond. Self-awareness enables us to build both of these attributes, each of which is so important for coaching: strong connections and positive challenges.

## Understanding your leadership style

### Leader's Shadow questions

There are a number of simple questions that can be used to develop self-awareness and to ensure that you or the person you are coaching has a congruent Leader's Shadow. Regularly asking yourself/your coachee some of the questions below will help you/your coachee to identify what you focus on:

- Where do you spend your time? What falls off your calendar?

- What questions do you frequently ask? What questions are never asked?

- What gets followed up? What is forgotten?

- What is important enough to call a meeting about? What isn't?

- At the end of meetings, what is or isn't emphasized? What language is used?

- Are you focusing on the right/best areas? Is this what you want to focus on?

- Does your focus cast the right Leader's Shadow?

- Is your shadow congruent – meaning are you aligned and consistent in what you say, act, prioritize and measure?

- What would your team say?

- What areas do you need to watch out for? Where are you vulnerable?

- Take the time to consider what shadow you cast. Is it the shadow you would like to cast or would you make changes? What changes would you make?

Other valuable questions to ask that will help your coachee (or you for that matter) develop greater self-awareness are outlined below.

### Understanding the real you

Crucially important for successful coaching is the ability to get right to the heart of who the person is – their behaviour, personality and world view. One of the deepest and most common pitfalls is believing you know everything about someone because you have inferred it from what you see. So, the individual is a successful CEO? They must be talented, driven, confident. They are young? They are probably lacking relevant experience and possibly confidence, too. Such assumptions are not only flawed but unhelpful. Even if these stereotypes are broadly true, generalizing about someone does little to help them. So, use these questions to develop a fuller picture of the person you are coaching. They are also valuable for self-coaching: getting to know the real *you*.

- Whom do you admire – and why? Who are your heroes?

- Whom do you dislike – and why?

- What do you want to do more, or better?

- What do you want to do less, or stop doing?

- When are you at your best and your worst?

- What is your greatest success?

- What have been the formative experiences during your life? (List the top three.)

- What experiences/roles/people have shaped your work and professional life?

- Who motivates you? What inspires you?

- What do you wish you could redo?

- What do you regret?

## Questions about You

- Whose opinions matter to you, and why?

- How well do you know yourself?

- What are you afraid of?

- What gives you energy?

- What do you enjoy most?

- What kind of person are you?

- What sort of person do you want to be?

- What qualities do you admire, and why?

- What gives you pleasure?

- What makes you tense?

- What is your greatest fear?

- What are your values? What qualities matter to you most?

- How reflective are you?

- What do you want to change or improve?

- What do you want to do that's different or new for you?

- What are your biggest challenges/concerns/priorities currently?

## You and the outside world

While the very nature of coaching is intrinsic – focusing on personal issues of behaviour, mindset and skills as well as broader personal issues such as relationships, decisions and goals – a vital element of coaching is the context in which it happens, and this is informed by other people. Coaching is never done in a vacuum, so keeping in mind relationships and other people is vital. The following questions will help both you and the coachee maintain that vital 'other' orientation.

- What do people need to know about you to work most effectively?

- How are you perceived by others? Are you sure about this – what evidence do you have?

- How would you describe yourself?

- How would your friends, family and work colleagues describe you? Are their descriptions – the adjectives they would use – similar and aligned? What would account for any differences?

- How and when do you cause negative feelings in others?

- What interpersonal skills do you need to develop or strengthen? Why? What evidence do you have (or what reason do you have) for strengthening these skills?

- What skills and attributes do you admire in others?

- What are you known for?

- How would you like your personal brand to develop – and why?

- How do you introduce yourself – in 30 seconds or less? (This is useful when networking and building your personal brand.)

## You and the future

Coaching is progressive and goal-oriented, and, as a result, questions that explore the future provide valuable context as well as a specific start to the coaching process.

- What do you aspire to achieve?

- Where do you see yourself in three years?

- What are your limiting beliefs – what holds you back?

- What advice would you give to your 18-year-old self?

## Your personal development

Questions that help someone look closely at their personal development needs are essential, not only in setting the tone for the discussion but also providing relevant insight and a practical starting point.

- Have you completed a psychometric assessment or 180/360-degree appraisal in the last two years? If so, how useful was it – what feedback or insights did you receive?

- Which skills and behaviours do you recognize and value most?

- Which areas are strengths for you – and where could you improve? Is this view shared by your colleagues?

- What are your strengths?

- What strengths can you develop further and make world-class?

- What strengths do you have that can be overplayed and become a weakness?

- What are your weaknesses or areas for development? What do you need/want to improve?

- What would you like to be your legacy? Your epitaph?

- Do you have a quote or philosophy that is particularly meaningful to you?

- Are you more creative or analytical? Do you favour intuition or analysis? How balanced is your approach?

- How agile, flexible and adaptive are you?

- How well do you cope with change, uncertainty or ambiguity?

## Your mindset

People with a *growth mindset* are keen to learn about fields that are outside their area of expertise; they make new and interesting connections and are progress-oriented in their style and approach. A growth mindset – a concept popularized by management writer Carol Dweck – is a hugely effective approach in a world of opportunity, challenge and change. Ask yourself/your coachee:

- Do you look to build on strengths and improve?

- Do you set your own standards, or do you seek approval from others?

- Can you effectively list and prioritize your challenges?

- Are you able to reframe – viewing challenges as opportunities?

- How often – and how well – do you step outside your comfort zone?

- Do you give and receive constructive feedback?

These questions matter: knowing what someone does well and where they can improve will enable them to focus and develop their effectiveness, skills, mindset and actions. It will also uncover strengths that can be further developed, as well as areas requiring improvement.

# CHAPTER 2

# Personal Effectiveness Questions

Working in a time of disruption, transformation and change requires resilience – not only for us individually but for colleagues and coachees as well. This chapter suggests questions to ask the coachee so they can develop greater resilience and adaptability, reduce stress, prioritize and set goals.

## Developing resilience and a positive growth mindset

Sometimes the greatest stress will come from an individual's own mind and the pressure they place on themselves when under pressure. Some people react to pressure with negativity, talking themselves into failure. To increase the coachee's positive mindset, ask:

- Do you possess a sufficiently positive mindset? Are you able to see either the inherent opportunities in a new situation, or accept its inevitability?

- Are you trying to be a perfectionist?

- Are you increasing stress levels by trying to deliver an exceptional outcome when acceptable is sufficient?

- Do you personalize outcomes or see yourself as the cause of a negative situation that is outside of your control, increasing your stress and frustration?

- Have you done enough to determine when it is necessary to deliver a perfect outcome, and when you need to let go?

- Are you unnecessarily personalizing outcomes?

- What is within your control? What is outside of your control?

- Do you engage in positive self-talk and maximize the positive?

- How often do you identify what you do well, not just what you don't do well?

- Do you congratulate yourself on your successes?

- Would it be useful to think more optimistically – imagine the best, rather than the worst? Sports psychologists encourage athletes to visualize success, as this then ensures a greater degree of focus.

## Being adaptable and preventing the causes of stress

Pressure at work is usually beneficial: it keeps us focused and productive. However, when pressure is too great it becomes stress, which has nothing but negative effects on us, our colleagues and the business. Being adaptable therefore means being able to recognize and prevent stress from emerging in the first place.

- Stress invariably builds up gradually over time and is all-consuming, being difficult to separate from normal behaviour. Stress is a personal matter, and the symptoms are either behavioural, physical or both. So, do you know when you are suffering from stress – or the danger of it?

- Are you aware of the behavioural symptoms of stress, and how these manifest in you? Symptoms include feeling worried, demotivated, irritated, withdrawn, upset, exhausted or weary, angry, misunderstood, frustrated and powerless.

- Are you aware of the consequences of stress? These include, for example, difficulties in concentrating, focusing, being creative, making decisions or solving problems.

- Do you accept that individual reactions to stress vary, and different people seem to have different levels at which they suffer from stress, based on their own personality and life experiences?

- In assessing your own level of stress do you understand your personal threshold for stress?

- Would it help to ask yourself whether this situation would normally upset you?

- Are you good at questioning your own pattern of behaviour – recognizing whether you are behaving as you would normally act (or react)? Would you have behaved that way last year? Is there something significant that is constantly on your mind?

- Can you distinguish typical patterns of behaviour from unusual ones? This matters, because one of the most common reactions to stress is the amplification of personality traits: for example, irritable people may become explosive, or quiet people become completely withdrawn.

- What more can you do to understand yourself? Specifically, can you further your understanding of what causes you stress, when you are likely to become stressed, and how you can avoid these situations?

- Are you taking or avoiding responsibility? Are you at risk of either denying the problem, in which case it will almost certainly worsen, or blaming someone (or something) else? Even if it is the fault of someone else, it is you who is being affected and you who needs to resolve it.

- Are you afraid, ashamed or uncertain to admit that you are suffering from stress? Keep in mind that the longer you delay, the worse the effects of the downward cycle become.

- Have you considered what is causing stress? Does it arise from your job, your role, your work relationships, change or something else, perhaps not work related at all?

- Are you doing enough to anticipate stressful periods (either at work or home) and plan for them?

- What strategies can you devise for handling stress? What may have worked for you in the past?

- How could you remove or reduce the cause of stress?

- Do you need to learn to accept the cause of stress if it cannot be removed?

- What techniques can you learn or develop to prevent or reduce stress? For example, time management and assertiveness are two of the most important skills in reducing and handling stress.

- Are you taking action to prevent, recognize and reduce stress in others?

- Is there a culture that leads to stress? For example, is there too much blaming, or too little communication or involvement? What changes would improve the culture and climate?

- Could you reduce stress by listening, without trying to 'make it OK' or smooth things over? Empathy is valuable – are you doing enough to let people know you are on their side?

- Would it be helpful to take a risk and move into the unknown, perhaps by trusting intuition, or drawing a line under contentious issues, perhaps by accepting responsibility?

- Are you or your colleagues at risk of shifting responsibility should things go wrong, or else avoid making the decision altogether?

## Developing your personal effectiveness

An essential skill for a leader at any level is the ability to focus on their own productivity, learning and results, and help others to do the same. This is the essence of objective setting, and it underpins a wide range of vital management skills – from team working and managing relationships to taking decisions and driving delivery.

- What are your motives and priorities for development? How do they fit with the business's strategy and objectives?

- What are your strengths and weaknesses – what should you be doing better, what future challenges are you likely to encounter?

- Who will you support your learning and development? Would a mentor or coach be useful?

- Have you devised your personal development plan?

- Do you maintain a learning journal or app to help you learn and develop?

- How will you apply what you have learned?

- How will you assess and measure your progress?

## Mastering the essentials: setting SMART personal and professional objectives

High-quality objectives or goals are usually SMART – as we saw in the introduction, this is an acronym meaning that they are specific (and stretching), measurable, achievable (and realistic), resourced (and relevant) and time-bound (and timely).

In addition, remember that goals come in two types: an *end goal*, which is an objective with a clear outcome or result (e.g. 'Complete project x by the end of the year') and a *performance goal*, which is usually ongoing and has the aim of making an improvement (e.g. 'Achieve better coaching and managing performance').

### Specific (and stretching)

It is important that the outcome is defined as clearly and positively as possible, so that the individual understands what is needed and is fully engaged with the task.

- Is the goal sufficiently specific, with the aim clearly understood?

- How will the person know they have succeeded?

- What will success look like?

- What will it take to succeed?

- Is the goal sufficiently stretching – how easy is it to accomplish?

- Will the goal help develop skills, understanding or confidence?

- Are there long-term or short-term benefits to the goal?

- Does the goal reflect the right priorities?

- What is the purpose or benefit of the goal – is the value of the outcome sufficiently clear and understood, especially by those who may need to support it?

- Is the goal engaging and exciting – does it motivate and excite?

- How will you approach the goal? What will you do first?

- Is this an end goal or a performance goal? Which is most appropriate?

## Measurable

People need to be able to understand when they are making progress in achieving their goal, and they need to know when it has been delivered.

- Is the goal measurable, with defined standards?

- What are the measures of success? How will you measure achievement?

- Specifically, what is the difference between a 'good' outcome and a 'great' outcome?

- Are the standards and measures widely recognized and agreed?

- Are the measures likely to be motivating, or dispiriting?

- How will it feel when the goal is achieved?

- Can you include measures that excite and encourage progress?

- Would it be useful to have interim measures on the road to achieving the goal?

## Achievable (and realistic)

Objectives which are difficult or impossible to achieve are pointless; the individual will fail, feel miserable and lose confidence (with implications for their future effectiveness), and the task will remain uncompleted. Alternatively, if the objective is easily achieved and lacks challenge, then it will fail to stimulate or develop the individual, as well as wasting their potential value. The key is to agree objectives that are stretching for the individual. In this way, the manager is establishing a virtuous cycle with stretching objectives being achieved and skills being developed, leading to greater enthusiasm and, as a result, an enhanced ability to accomplish other objectives in the future.

- Is the objective achievable and realistic, with an appropriate amount of 'stretch'?

- What might hinder progress?

- What will be the toughest, most challenging aspect?

- What will be the easiest aspect of progressing the goal?

- How will achievement be recognized and rewarded?

- What will you do (personally) once you have achieved your goal?

- Are you experienced and effective at goal setting? Might your goal be subject to biases, perhaps as fundamental as innate optimism or pessimism, and how will you guard against these?

Would it be useful, perhaps for other people, to keep a record or learning journal of your progress?

## Resourced (and relevant)

An essential aspect of objective setting is ensuring that the individual completing the task has the necessary resources and options to succeed. If the objective is under-resourced, then the result will be a lack of progress and a sense of frustration.

The key is to discuss and quantify the resources that are needed and agree with the individual where these will be found. If resources are lacking, then options or contingencies will need to be agreed when the objective is being set. What matters at this stage is that the individual possesses the initiative and drive to either secure the necessary resources or find a way of succeeding without them, and that the manager is fully supportive.

- What resources do you need?

- In an ideal world, what resources would you need to easily achieve your goal?

- How and where will you obtain these resources?

- Is there the necessary support to achieve the goal?

- Whose buy-in do you need to accomplish the goal?

- How does the goal connect with other goals or activities – would it help to include your work as part of a broader project, activity or initiative?

- How would you describe the benefit and impact of successfully achieving your goal to someone who may be unfamiliar with this activity?

- What is your 'elevator pitch' to explain the goal and make sure that it has sufficient support? Is this compelling and engaging?

- Key resources are typically: people, time, money, publicity/awareness, and something specific to your context (e.g. if you are developing a new app, then technology expertise is helpful; if you are designing a recruitment process, then experience of people management is helpful).

- Where, specifically, would additional resources have the greatest benefit?

## Time-bound (and timely)

A deadline, plan or critical path with milestones is a great way of focusing an individual's work and giving them the necessary impetus and momentum to succeed. 'Time' actually has two meanings when setting goals: first, it can mean *time-bound* – constrained by a deadline; second, it can mean *timely* – delivered at the right (most appropriate) time.

- Is this the right goal at the right time?

- When will you complete the goal? Is there a 'drop-dead' date by which the goal must be achieved?

- Is your goal scheduled?

- When will the goal start?

- What will be your first step?

- How long will be needed?

- Would your goal benefit from a false end date, or a provisional end date at which time you receive feedback and can make further refinements?

- How long will it take to achieve?

- What are the milestones along the way to achieving the goal?

- Does your timescale match expectations? Is everyone agreed with your planned timescale?

## Other questions when goal setting

When it comes to goal setting, two great quotes are useful to keep in mind. The first insight, from writer Lewis Carroll, is that, 'If you don't where you are going any road will do.' In other words, goals are essential for channelling and focusing our work. The second insight is from the Italian artist Michelangelo: 'The greater danger for most of us lies not in setting our aim too high and falling short, but in setting our aim too low, and achieving our mark.' If they are to propel us forward, goals need to be *challenging*.

If you are writing the objectives (and especially if you are writing them for someone else), have you used the right language and tone?

Is the language you use about your goal – whether written or spoken, sufficiently positive, clear, free of jargon and dynamic – using the active voice? Or, to put it another way, have you ensured that the language used is not confusing, ambiguous and demotivating?

- Would it help to write objectives in the first person and the present tense, in a way that is practical and uses active words (e.g. 'achieve', 'obtain', 'develop', 'organize')?

- Are you sufficiently positive about the benefits of the objective?

- Have you taken into account and mitigated the risks of pursuing this goal?

- Would it be useful to check for any unintended consequences (common sense is vital and assumed)? Who and what will be directly affected by your objective?

- Is the individual who is progressing the goal taking sufficient personal responsibility?

- Is the goal sufficiently developmental, enabling an individual to learn and improve?

- Does the goal play to people's strengths?

- Does the goal align with other goals and activities?

- Would it help to use the STAR (Situation, Task, Actions/ Activities, Results) approach when setting goals for someone else? STAR is an acronym which focuses the goal-setter on:
  ◦ explaining the current *Situation* and priorities
  ◦ outlining the *Task* to be completed
  ◦ identifying the *Actions* or *Activities* that are needed
  ◦ describing the ideal *Result*.

## Developing SMART objectives

Detailed below is a practical set of questions designed to help your coachee (or you) develop SMART objectives.

- Are you clear about and committed to the outcome or result you are looking to achieve?

- Do you want the outcome enough to work consistently for it? If not, what would it take for you to be sufficiently motivated?

- Is this outcome written down?

- Does this outcome align with other people or activities?

- Is the desired outcome sufficiently positive? (E.g. 'I want to enjoy greater influence' rather than 'I want to stop being ignored'.)

- Are you moving towards something exciting, or are you moving away from something negative? (It is usually more motivating to move towards a positive than away from a negative.)

- Have you avoided referring to negative things?

- Have you considered what resources or experience you already have to help you achieve your outcome? This may include life experience, skills or personal qualities.

- Do you understand what can be controlled? Is it in your power alone? If not, where do you have control and where does control or influence rest with others?

- Is the desired outcome sufficiently specific and focused?

- When will you start and finish?

- What will success look like?

- What will you actually see, hear and feel that convinces you of success? (For some people, what they hear may include internal dialogue.)

- When will you systematically review this outcome?

- If it is a long-term outcome, how often will you revisit it?

- How would someone else know you have achieved it?

- Are you using the best of the present situation?

- Are you learning from experience? Is there more you can do to incorporate the past and present into your planned outcome?

- Have you mapped the likely sequence of events, stages or milestones?

- Is this goal what you specifically want, or is it a way of getting something else that is important to you? If it is the latter, are there other ways of getting it? Do you need to set smaller, intermediate outcomes? Is all the useful detail written down clearly? Most importantly, what is the next step?

The ability to set clear objectives and see them through is a defining management skill. Without doubt, achieving objectives for yourself and your team members will help you be more effective and successful.

# CHAPTER 3

# Emotional Intelligence Questions

Emotional intelligence is a person's ability to acquire and apply knowledge from their emotions and the emotions of others, so they can be more successful and lead a more fulfilling life. Its value lies in enabling us to sense and use emotions, helping us to manage ourselves and build positive, productive relationships.

Psychologist Daniel Goleman popularized his view of emotional intelligence in the 1995 bestseller *Emotional Intelligence: Why It Can Matter More than IQ*. Building on the work of Howard Gardner and Peter Salovey, Goleman highlighted the fact that emotions are critical in determining a leader's success. In times of change, pressure or crisis, possessing emotional intelligence is an advantage as success is determined by recognizing, understanding and dealing with emotions. For example, we may all feel anger but emotional intelligence means knowing what to do with the emotion of anger to achieve the best outcome.

Emotional intelligence is evident in five areas:

1. Knowing one's emotions

2. Managing emotions

3. Motivating people

4. Recognizing emotions in others

5. Handling relationships.

These emotional competencies build on each other in a hierarchy. At the bottom of this hierarchy (competency 1) is the ability to identify one's emotional state. Some knowledge of competency 1 is needed to move to the next competency. Likewise, knowledge or skill in the first three competencies is needed to show empathy, read and influence positively other people's emotions (competency 4). The first four competencies lead to increased ability to enter and sustain good relationships (competency 5).

The key issues and priorities when developing emotional intelligence, therefore, are to:

- understand which of these five areas you can strengthen or improve

- move effectively between each of these five areas

- recognize the specific areas where others can improve

- help others improve where this is needed, and help them move between competencies.

## Building connection, understanding and rapport

The following questions – which can be directed towards both yourself – the coach – and your coachee – focus on developing warmth, connection and rapport. These are vital prerequisites as they enable the coach or leader to challenge the coachee positively.

- How warm and open are you?

- Do you have sufficient empathy? When (in what circumstances) do you find it hard to display empathy?

- How much attention do you pay to relationships?

- Which relationships do you value – and why?

- What are the most significant *professional* relationships in your life?

- What are the most significant *personal* relationships in your life?

- Which relationships could you improve?

- What more can you do to develop key relationships? How will you develop them?

- How are you perceived when you first meet someone?

- Are you warm when you greet someone – could you be warmer?

- Do you always greet people warmly and connect with them, even when you know them well?

- In what circumstances are you cooler towards someone?

- Do you know someone who is warm and assertive? How do they make you feel?

- Do you know someone who is cold and 'stand-offish'? How do they make you feel?

- What level of warmth is appropriate for your context, culture and people you are working with?

- Are you ever too warm – possibly overfamiliar? If so, when?

- Do you overuse humour when you meet someone? People often do, especially when nervous.

- Are you genuinely interested in connecting with new people? This matters if you want to lead, work through people, and develop your influence.

## Questions to build someone's emotional intelligence

These questions broadly focus on the five elements of emotional intelligence: knowing one's own emotions, managing emotions, motivating and engaging people, recognizing emotions in others, and handling relationships.

- How are you feeling?

- What's on your mind?

- When are you... [*insert the emotion or feeling that would be most relevant for the individual – e.g.* most in control/happiest/worried]?

- What are your triggers? What are the things that set you off?

- What are your dominant emotions?

- What emotions would you like to dial up or experience more often?

- Which emotions do you need to manage more or better?

- How do emotions typically affect you?

- How are you with emotional people? For example, do they bring out the best in you?

- Are you an introvert or extrovert? Do you get your energy from facts, analysis and reflection, or from people, activities and events?

- How well do you manage your emotions?

- Do you always manage your emotions effectively?

- When did you last... [*choose the most appropriate emotion – e.g.* cry/lose your temper/laugh, or feel joy/terror/excitement/ fulfilment/happiness/pleased/hesitation/trepidation/calmness/ nervousness]?

- When were you last 'in the flow' or 'in the zone' – meaning working at your absolute best and absolutely flying?

- What did it feel like to be working at your best? How did it happen? How can you replicate that feeling?

- How well do you manage and control your emotions? Could you do this more?

- How effectively do you express and show your emotions? Could you do this more?

- Are you good at motivating, engaging or inspiring people? What makes you successful at this? OR How could you do this better?

- Would it help to be more or less emotional?

- Emotions are often context-specific: do you always choose the right emotion at the right time? Could this improve? When did you do this well, and when did you not?

- How open and engaging are you? Do you value openness and engage in open discussions?

- Do you listen actively – meaning intently and effectively? Are you a good listener – could this improve? What evidence do you have that you do/do not listen well?

- How well do you question and explore the views of others?

- How willing are you to amend or alter your view based on someone's feedback or suggestions?

- Thinking of colleagues/a specific colleague: which of their emotions and behaviours do you value, and why? Which behaviours irritate you, and why?

- Passionate people are often really effective at engaging others: are you passionate?

- What are you passionate about?

- How effectively do you convey your passions? When does this happen?

- Could you be better and more open at sharing your passions/the things that matter to you?

- How well do people know you?

- Do you deploy your emotions in the best way, or do they control you? Could you improve the way you handle your emotions?

- Could you do more to draw people towards you?

## Questions for someone lacking self-awareness

Most leaders and experienced coaches have been in the difficult position of managing someone who thinks their performance is terrific when it's not. If you fail to address the situation, the person's work won't improve. Several techniques can help:

- Start by being clear about expectations and pointing out specific areas to work on. For example: 'What do you think could improve?'; 'Where do you see the greatest priority for development or change?'

- Counter-intuitively perhaps, consider 'opening them up' by recognizing what they do well. This then provides you, as a coach, with both the permission and opportunity to surprise them with the impact of their actions or behaviour.

- If you are their leader, set aside some time to mentor, supervise and constructively help your employee recognize their deficits. This doesn't mean micromanaging them – you're simply making sure they have the resources and support to do their job.

- Be discerning with praise. It's important to recognize their good work, but overstating their performance runs the risk of sending mixed messages.

Finally, and most significantly of all, use questioning as a way of building an individual's understanding of themselves and increasing their self-awareness. For example:

- What do you sometimes think of saying or doing but don't?

- How will you remember your strengths in times of confrontation?

- How would you feel if you walked away from this?

- What is your greatest fear?

- How easy is it for you to say no?

- How are you going to find time to do this?

- What do you really want?

- How will you maintain your own equilibrium?

- What are the low/medium-risk situations to try out this new behaviour?

- How will you build early successes/alliances?

- How are you going to rehearse the behaviour before going live?

- Who in this group could help you?

- How can you stop 'hoping'?

- How good are you at taking advice?

- How much of yourself do you give to others?

- How do you show your appreciation for others? Could you do it more directly?

- How can you put involvement of others more central to your thinking?

- What will help you push harder?

- How are you colluding with your own unhappiness?

- What makes you combative at the moment?

- What are you learning (and therefore risking)? What are you risking (and therefore learning)?

- How would I know what you are feeling without asking?

- How would I know that you trust me?

- How do you build your credibility?

- Do you lead or do you respond to the lead given?

- How can you stop getting caught in the middle, while still moving the issue forward?

- How much time and thought do you give to influencing?

- What do you need to do now (because if you don't it will go wrong)?

- What do you need to do that, once you have done it, will make you relieved?

- How will you engage someone's heart? That is, how will you connect with someone and get them on board?

- How well do you delegate work?

- What does it feel like to let someone in to your world? Do you do this easily, often or well?

- How deliberate are your actions and planning?

- Are your strengths sometimes overplayed, potentially becoming a liability?

- What could you say about yourself that would help others understand you more personally?

- How can you make your position clearer?

- What does courage mean for you?

- How do you want to be remembered?

- What will you regret not doing?

- What can you do to relax before you enter new situations?

- How can you make sure you draw attention to your strengths?

- Do you need to be gentler on yourself?

- What can you do to remember your proud achievements?

- Do you ever say, 'This isn't for me'?

## Conflict-related questions

Many of the relationship challenges and issues presented to coaches reflect a desire on the part of the coachee to either improve relationships generally, or to improve a specific dysfunctional relationship. One of the biggest issues here is to help the coachee find the courage to address the issue appropriately, in a way that is timely, sensitive, fair and effective.

- Are you sufficiently sensitive to the feelings of others? Could this be improved?

- How do you typically defuse a conflict in your team/with your boss/with this person?

- What is the source/what are the causes of this conflict?

- When does conflict typically occur? OR When did this conflict begin?

- What are the underlying issues causing the conflict – not the specific issues, but the other intangibles? For example, is there a clash of style? A resentment over a past issue or event? A culture clash? A mutual lack of understanding? Something else?

- Do you call out difficult or antagonistic behaviour when you see it? If not, why not? If so, what happens?

- Do you know this person's triggers – the things that upset them? Do they know yours?

- What more could you do to avoid or pre-empt conflict?

- What could you do to resolve a current conflict?

- What action could you take to resolve or address a past conflict or lingering resentment?

When it comes to emotions, relationships and conflict in particular, courage is what is really required. The ability to see the issue dispassionately and calmly, and to engage with it in a practical and committed way.

# CHAPTER 4

# Learning Questions

## Learning and development at work

The greatest coaches and managers are characterized by a restless desire to learn, develop and improve. This keeps their skills and outlook current, relevant and flexible.

Closely linked to this is the fact that coaches and managers need to take personal responsibility for delivering the results that are needed. As a manager, you know that the environment and prevailing conditions, including the effectiveness of people in your team, are likely to change. The only solution is to be engaged, positive and constructive, finding ways to manage the situation and to:

1. understand current reality

2. remain self-aware, open and flexible

3. develop capability and mindset.

The questions throughout this chapter focus on enabling the coach/ leader to help their coachee learn; they recognize that learning is best achieved when there is a context, the opportunity for reflection and a desire to learn. Some of the questions, however, may be directly for the coach.

## 1 Understanding the current reality

- What skills do you need to develop to succeed in your current role?

- What skills do you need to succeed in the future? What new developments are taking place in your industry or organization that require you to develop new skills?

- What do you do well? What strengths do you have that could be made world-class?

- What are the things that you need to know?

What do you need to do more or better?

## 2 Remaining self-aware, open and flexible

Thinking about the certainties of the past, what has changed, or is changing? And what do you need to unlearn? Remember the words of the American writer Mark Twain (reputedly): 'It ain't what you don't know that gets you into trouble. It's what you know for sure that just ain't so.'

- Who do you trust that you can go to for guidance and advice?

- Whose feedback do you value?

- What could you do to increase the quality, quantity, value or impact of the feedback you receive?

- Who would you choose to be your mentor?

- Who can keep your thinking current about key issues?

## 3 Developing capability and mindset

- How will you learn and develop new skills?

- What is your learning style – your preferred way of learning?

- Where do you see yourself (what role will you have) in 12 months, two years and five years, respectively? What are the changes you need to achieve and the skills you need to develop to succeed in the future?

## Avoiding potential pitfalls when learning and developing

There are three potential pitfalls when assessing your own skills and behaviour as a coach or manager. As well as improving your own self-awareness, this information will allow you to help others overcome these flaws.

### Regarding a personal failing as a situational problem

Even experienced managers can believe that problems are a result of a situation rather than a consequence of their own inaction or failures. Attempting to resolve a situational problem is seen as more acceptable than overcoming a personal shortcoming, so that is where many people focus, projecting blame onto the situation. This is a mistake and will only perpetuate the problem. To avoid this pitfall, ask yourself: do these difficulties result from the situation or from my attitudes and approach? If the answer to this question is to be of any use, you must strive to be ruthlessly honest, methodical, analytical and objective.

### Avoiding the new and unfamiliar

Coaches, especially when they are new to a role, are often attracted to tasks they feel comfortable with, avoiding those issues where they don't. Activity in areas that are familiar is a common way to avoid action in other, unfamiliar areas. This can mean that opportunities are being missed simply because they lie outside an individual's comfort zone. What matters is tackling the right issues, not simply acting.

## Suppressing doubts and acting with certainty

A frequent response to the demands of a new or challenging situation is to suppress your uncertainties and doubts by acting with certainty and in a commanding manner. While it is important to project a confident image, the need to be seen to be in control can lead you to suppress opinions and can result in weak or flawed decisions.

## Strengths-based development questions

When people are evaluated on their strengths they are challenged to take responsibility for them and hone them to perfection. For that reason alone it is a great place for coaches and managers to start when developing accountability and delivering results.

It is worth noting that the topic of strengths-based development is discussed by Sally Bibb in *The Strengths Book: Discover How to be Fulfilled in Your Work and in Life*.

Ask your coachee the following questions:

### Awareness

- How well do you understand and appreciate your strengths?

- What are you good at?

- What do you enjoy?

- Would feedback (focusing on what you do well) be useful?

- Are there any hidden strengths – for example, activities that require specific and valuable skills?

## Application

- Where, when and how often do you apply your strengths?

- What more can you do to increase and expand their application?

## Amplify

- How and when could you share your expertise and multiply the use of your strengths?

- Could you help to develop others?

## Add to

- What would help you go deeper and further in the way you use your strengths?

- How can you add to your strengths?

- The challenge is not moving from good to great – it's moving from great to world-class. What would that take to achieve?

## Developing leadership skills and mindset: the Self-Development Cycle

Sometimes, achieving an objective requires an individual to develop their skills or acquire new ones. The Self-Development Cycle is a method of focusing, planning and undertaking development activities in a rigorous, thorough and practical way. The success of the Self-Development Cycle depends on setting clear objectives and repeating the planning process regularly (at least every year, preferably every six months or when circumstances change, such as taking on a new role). Below I give the key questions relating to each of the seven stages of the cycle.

The Leadership Cycle

## 1 Establish the purpose

You need to keep the overall aim firmly in mind and then ensure that all activities directly support this aim. Without this clear goal in mind it is often difficult to stay on track, keep momentum or maintain motivation.

- What are the areas of greatest opportunity and need for your development?

- Why is your personal development important to you now?

- What will 'good' look like?

## 2 Identify development needs

These must be identified and a programme for meeting those needs should be devised. In particular, the needs must be realistic and time-constrained, with a definite deadline.

- What are the top three priorities for your development? Why are these significant?

- What is the timeframe for development?

## 3 Look at your opportunities for development

Deciding how to meet the development needs is the next stage, and this may include a mix of formal and informal methods. As well as effectiveness, cost and timing, bear in mind your own preferred learning style: what approach suits you best?

- How will you develop your skills?

- How will you develop the right thinking and mindset needed for the future?

- How will you blend formal and informal learning and development?

- What can you learn from your colleagues and those around you?

## 4 Devise an action plan

This will be necessary for more complex development needs that require a range of activities or an ongoing process. You should also consider how the development process will be supported.

- Who will provide your learning and development?

- How will you learn and grow?

- Who will keep you on track – for example, by providing support, challenges, feedback?

- Is your development plan SMART – are your goals specific, measurable, achievable, resourced/relevant and time-bound/ timely (see Chapter 2)?

## 5 Undertake development

This is the core of the process.

- Great learning needs a context; or, put another way, it is hard to learn without a context. So, why does learning and development matter to you and the organization now? What is happening that makes this development timely, relevant and valuable? Is that clearly and widely understood?

- How will the results be integrated into workplace activities?

- Are you ready and committed to applying your learning?

- How will you manage your time?

- What will you stop doing to make time for: a) learning activities and b) new habits?

- How much time are you setting aside for reviewing, reflecting and discussing your learning? (Reflection is an important part of learning.)

- What is your learning style – and what are the implications of this style for your routine, time and colleagues?

- Whose support do you need?

## 6 Record outcomes

Keep track of development activities in order to assess results against planned objectives.

What is the best way to review progress? How will you assess what methods work best for you, and take these further?

## 7 Review and evaluate

The process of recording and evaluating will help to assess the extent to which the original objective has been achieved. The development manager may suggest including this assessment as part of the individual's development plan.

- Are you updating your development plan and keeping in future activities?

- How will you share your skills and learning with colleagues? Can you cascade your learning – potentially create a movement?

## Questions to support personal development

- Finally, what more can you do to create a learning environment – a place where people routinely learn, provide mutual support, and value personal development?

- What are your motives and priorities for development? How do they fit with the business's strategy and objectives?

- What are your strengths and weaknesses? What should you be doing better? What future challenges are you likely to encounter?

- Who will support your learning and development? Would a mentor or coach be useful?

- Have you devised your personal development plan?

- Do you maintain a learning journal or app to help you learn and develop?

- How will you apply what you have learned?

- How will you assess and measure your progress?

# CHAPTER 5

# The Toughest Questions

## How to Shift Mindset and Behaviour

The best way to develop someone's mindset and behaviour depends, of course, on the individual and, to a lesser extent, their context. That said, several practical tools can help: highlighting insights from data, inviting third-party feedback, encouraging self-reflection, investigating their impact on other people, exploring personal goals, priorities and aspirations, appealing to their personal motivations, providing guidance and example, offering practical experiences and, in particular, removing or reducing barriers and limiting beliefs. Succeeding with all of these techniques requires a thoughtful, practical, questioning approach.

Crucially, when coaching someone to help them change their behaviour it is important to remember that people typically find it easier to move *towards* something positive than to move *away* from something negative. So, first help the person look for the goal they want to achieve, and take time to explore why they want this goal, what it means to them, how it will make things better. Where possible, encourage the person, enthuse them. Useful questions to ask include:

- How will you feel when (not 'if') this goal is achieved?

- Who will benefit? How?

- What does achieving this goal mean to you? How will you feel?

- Why is it important?

- What are the implications, benefits or consequences of accomplishing this goal?

- What will 'good' look like?

- What will success enable you to do that you can't do now?

## Using data, assessments and tools

Many tools have their own specific focus and power. For example, the popular FIRO-B instrument focuses on the nature of interpersonal relations (FIRO-B is an acronym for Fundamental Interpersonal Relations Orientation-Behavior, and is based on the work of American psychologist William Schutz). The tool helps individuals understand their behaviour and the behaviour of others, and it is used by coaches to help an individual improve understanding of their interpersonal needs and, as a result, helping improve their workplace interactions. FIRO-B is one tool among many. The best ones have a clear focus, a proven track record, and either a sound basis in psychological research, or a simple transparent approach. For example, a 360-degree assessment is not necessarily psychologically rigorous, but it is clear, simple and transparent, as well as proven.

Also remember that insights from data can be flawed – for example, they may be based on incomplete or flawed information – and it is generally best to regard them as feedback – a 'snapshot' of someone that may be temporary and fixed rather than dynamic or long-lasting. The rules of feedback should, of course, apply:

1. Treat the insights as a gift

2. Don't be defensive

3. Look for the reasons behind the comments, not simply the comments themselves

4. Say 'thank you', ask for clarification, explore the issue, think about it further or make a change (or a combination of these responses!).

Key questions for coaches to consider include questions that delve deeper into the data provided by the tool. In addition, it can help to ask:

- How do you feel?

- What do you think of the results?

- What actions do you want to take as a result of this feedback?

- What changes would you like to achieve?

- Are there times or specific circumstances when this behaviour is dominant?

- What are the alternatives to this behaviour?

## Harnessing the power of feedback

Inviting feedback is a great way of showing openness, inspiring trust and developing leadership style and approach. For some people, though admittedly not everyone, it can also have the effect of opening their eyes in such a revelatory way that their desire to change is accelerated.

Feedback involves targeting specific people, being specific about where their input is wanted, and being open about why. It is particularly important to avoid becoming defensive or arguing with the comments; instead, the individual should reflect on it carefully and decide whether to act.

- What do you see as my strengths?

- What do you think is my greatest strength?

- What do you think I can do more, better and differently?

- What do you wish I did more or less of?

- What do you appreciate most in your interactions with me?

- What do you think went well?

- What can I do to improve my rating in this area next year?

- What can I do to be more helpful to people on the team?

- What are your most important goals for next year?

- How can I support your work?

## Encouraging self-reflection

Self-reflection helps most people – even those who are particularly confident or possess large egos – to focus on their behaviour, the changes they want to achieve, and – crucially – the reasons why they want to achieve them.

- How do you feel?

- What do you want to change?

- Then explore this question further, for example, by asking:

- Why do you want to change?
- What will it mean to you to change?
- How will you achieve this? What will you do differently?
- When will you see the results – what's the timescale?

Other questions that encourage self-reflection include:

- Of the things you want to change, what do you want to change most? (And why? How? When?)

- What are your dominant emotions?

- Who has most profoundly affected you – and how did they affect you?

- What is the most significant event in your life?

- What is your philosophy or approach to life?

- What is your goal, your purpose?

- What drives and motivates you?

- What gives you energy?

- What drains you of energy?

- What frustrates or saddens you?

- Where do you see yourself in five years? Ten years?

- What would you like your obituary to read?

- What do people think of you?

- Who are your greatest influences?

- What qualities do you admire?

- What are your dreams, your aspirations?

- What are your strengths?

- How often do you use your strengths?

- What do you enjoy?

- What do you dislike?

- How much of your time is spent doing things you enjoy/value/ do well?

- How much of your time is spent doing things you dislike/don't value/do poorly?

- What strengths do you have that you could make world-class?

- What strengths do you have that could be overplayed?

- What are the priority areas for improvement?

- What is your greatest achievement?

- How did you accomplish your greatest achievement – what was involved?

- What is your biggest disappointment?

- How do people relate to you?

- What do people like about you, what do you think they would want to change?

- Who are your best friends, your confidants – the people who you value and who you listen to?

- What is your reputation?

- What achievements or events are you known for?

- How would you like to change your reputation?

- What limiting beliefs do you have?

- When – and why – do you lack confidence? Does this need to change?

- How do you learn?

- What type of person are you?

- What type of person do you want to be?

## Investigating a person's impact on other people

There are many ways of assessing how a person comes across. A good starting point is for the person to reflect on their personality and experiences. In particular, it helps to ask: What are your:

- key relationships?

- strengths?

- successes?

- the things you are known for (i.e. your reputation)?

- personal and professional goals?

- needs?

- values?

- priorities?

- dominant emotions?

The following questions may also be helpful:

- How do people typically behave around you?

- What surprises you about the behaviour of those around you – and why?

- How would close friends describe you?

- How would people who don't know you well regard you – what label might they use, and is this fair or accurate?

- What would you like colleagues and contacts to do more, less or better?

These questions will then start to build up a picture of how others see and experience the person. Next, help them begin to think about what might need to change.

## Exploring personal goals, priorities and aspirations

Achieving clarity about an individual's personal goals and aspirations is not only valuable (essential, in fact) for achieving those goals; it is also illuminating – highlighting an individual's preferences and where their focus and energy tend to go. An exploration of these issues is therefore vitally important.

- What are your personal priorities?

- What goals do you want to achieve?

- Why these goals?

- How committed are you to achieving them?

- How will you achieve them?

- How will you maintain progress to achieving these goals?

- What would help you achieve them?

- How do these goals fit with the broader picture? What connects your goals?

- Who does these things well already? Who can help you, who can you learn from?

## Understanding personal motivations

Understanding an individual's motivations is hugely significant and valuable as a coach, enabling the coach/manager to help their coachee find their flow, the actions, behaviours and climate that will help ensure that the individual thrives and succeeds.

- What gets you out of bed in the morning?

- What drives you?

- What sustains you during challenging times?

- Where do you get your energy, your focus, your motivation?

- What drains your energy?

- What is your best kind of day?

- What are your derailers, your saboteurs – the things that can send you off course or cause frustration?

- What is your worst kind of day?

- What have been the top three drivers of success for you during your career?

- What motivates and shapes your private life?

- How do you want to be seen?

- What do you want to be known for?

- How would you like to be remembered?

- Where do you want to be this time next year?

- Where do you want to be in five or ten years?

- What do you want to achieve?

- If you are successful, what will that look and feel like? How will you know?

The value of this line of questioning is that the coachee will focus on their personal motivations and goals, reinforcing – or reminding – someone that they can change and that change and progress are valuable, and then specifically getting them to think about *how* and *why* they need to develop.

## Finding examples and benefiting from experience

A useful next step is often to provide guidance, encouragement and examples, and bring to bear the power of experience. The following questions can help.

- How feasible is your goal?

- What might get in the way of success?

- What can you do about potential blockers or challenges?

- What do you need to know, do and believe in order to succeed?

- What would help?

- Whose support do you need?

- Who can you learn from? Who can you discuss this goal with?

- What do you need to avoid?

- What lessons from other people or situations would benefit you?

- Why do you believe this goal is achievable?

## Removing or reducing barriers and limiting beliefs

Finally, it helps to look deeper and pay attention to any limiting beliefs. Some of the most common limiting beliefs are:

- fear of success/greatness/failure/unworthiness

- fear that we are not good enough to achieve what we want

- fear that we are unpopular/unloved/lacking the positive support of others (or incapable of these things)

- fear that we will be rejected (typically leading the individual to avoid relationships or to adopt appeasing behaviours)

- fear that negative and possibly stereotypical attributes will be assigned

- fear that change or progress is too hard and huge, and that daunting amounts of effort will be required

- fear that you lack the support of others who will, instead, hold you back.

The key to success as a coach is to help the individual, your coachee, observe and describe the thoughts that reveal their beliefs. Several questions can help get this process started – and it is really important, too, that this is an exploratory conversation full of support, challenge and positive intent.

- Is how you talk to yourself helping you or holding you back?

- What are your limiting beliefs?

- Do you still believe this [*the limiting belief or issue*] to be true? If so, why? What evidence do you have?

- Can you find any instances where what you believe is not always true?

- Are you willing to at least try to embrace an opposite belief?

- Could this belief come from a past event that you mistakenly assigned meaning to?

- What do you have going for you? What is it about you that will ensure success?

- Where do your views about you come from?

- Regardless of the past, how valid are your views *today*?

Crucially, once your coachee identifies a limiting belief, they can release it and replace it with a more constructive, accurate and supportive belief that will serve them better. It is a liberating feeling that will not only drive them forward but also help instil confidence and belief, making a profound difference in many ways.

## How to instil belief and banish the impostor

Imposter syndrome is when we feel unworthy, overpromoted, perhaps, or simply unqualified to do something. The truth is that everyone occasionally suffers from imposter syndrome, even the most senior executives. Three techniques can help whenever you or your coachee feel like you're an impostor, lacking in self-belief:

1. Recognize the advantages and reframe

2. Adopt a learning mindset: be curious, question and learn

3. Understand that it's normal: you're not alone

Such feelings – and the solutions to them – may also apply to your coachee, of course, so this section may also be relevant to them.

### Recognize the advantages and reframe

There are positives to being new in your field. When you're not an expert in the issue, situation or conventional wisdom, you can ask questions that haven't been asked before and approach issues in new an inventive ways.

- What unique perspectives and experiences do you bring to the role? What are your strengths?

- What excites you about the role? Why are you suited to it?

- What aspects of the role are you looking forward to?

- What part of your role are you pleased about and grateful or thankful for?

- What are your concerns, and in what circumstances might these concerns actually be useful?

- How reasonable are your concerns? Could your concerns be at least partly driven by a lack of confidence, a bad experience or limiting beliefs? If so, how can those concerns be overcome now and into the future?

### Adopt a learning mindset: be curious, question and learn

Focus more on what you're learning rather than on how you're performing. Don't beat yourself up for making mistakes. Appreciate that your limitations and missteps are helping you develop.

- Are you sufficiently open-minded, curious and ready to learn? How could you proactively put this curiosity into action?

- There are sure to be unfamiliar or new things you need to learn, know or do – what are they, and how will you get up to speed?

- What do you need to unlearn?

- What do you need to let go?

- What aspect of your role do you think might need changing?

- Where are the biggest opportunities – the low-hanging fruit?

- What are your priorities? Are they sufficiently well-known and agreed?

- What are the things about the new role that seem surprising, suboptimal, in need of questioning or improving?

- Where do you personally want to improve?

- What personal strengths do you need to rely on?

- What potential weaknesses do you need to guard against?

## Understand that it's normal: you're not alone

In a time of complexity, challenge and change, it is inevitable that you will encounter the unfamiliar, or people who are much more expert than you, and if you have any emotional intelligence and empathy at all, you will inevitably feel like an imposter – at least occasionally. Remember, the chances are that others in your situation feel the exact same way.

- What are the most important and valuable relationships for you to develop?

- What are the most important sources of information?

- How will you fit, and what will you change?

- How will you sustain your focus, energy and your spirits? How will you stay the course when things are uncertain or pressured?

- Who can you learn from?

As a coach facing a person who is suffering from imposter syndrome, you should remember that people can often focus on their priorities or their new role or team without actually appreciating how rare and valuable their skills are, or how good they are at what they do. Of course, there are many other people with no shortage of hubris or ego and who consider themselves superb, at least, for most of the time. Whatever the reality, several points are clear about people who worry about being 'found out'. In particular:

- **Executives feel insecure and worried about their own competence** – in which case, is this reasonable? Why is this so? Is such a concern feasible or fanciful?

- **Executives value their own personal effectiveness and success** – they're serious about doing well. In this case, the question for the coach is how best to build on this desire for self-awareness, improvement and success?

Other useful questions to consider include:

- What evidence does the person you are coaching have to support their feelings? Why do they feel this way?

- How likely and feasible are their concerns? What's the worst that could happen?

- Is it the case that there's simply a gap between where the individual's skills, knowledge or experience are at the moment, and where they need to be in the future? If so, how can this gap be managed?

### Questions to build confidence and self-belief

When faced with a person who lacks confidence and self-belief, it is useful to break this challenge down into several key issues:

- Recognizing and resolving limiting beliefs (see questions above)

- Overcoming the fear of risk

- Creating a positive climate

- Developing boldness and audacious thinking.

- Useful questions for the three remaining issues are listed below.

## Overcoming the fear of risk

Fear of any sort needs to be explored and made explicit, and in business, particularly, a fear of risk can be limiting – especially as risk is often inevitable. The solution is to explore, understand, make explicit and, ideally, share the key issues and fears.

- What are you worried about?

- What is your biggest concern?

- What's the worst that could happen?

- Why does this concern you?

- What is the benefit – the reason for making this change?

- What is the risk of inaction?

- How can you both mitigate and manage this risk?

- What would you need to believe to overcome this fear?

- Who could succeed with this issue – what would they do?

- What mindset is needed to succeed?

- Break it down – remember the Chinese proverb: The journey of a thousand miles starts with a single step. So, what steps do you need to take?

- How will you prepare?

- What will you do first?

- What are the milestones?

- How rational are your fears?

- Could it be possible that you are overemphasizing these fears?

## Creating a positive climate

If we are to be audacious ourselves and expect others to follow, then there are several techniques to use, proactively and determinedly, to ensure success. These are not intended as a linear process but rather techniques and areas of focus that are important at specific moments when we are pushing back the boundaries of risk and audacity. This includes:

Being clear about what we need to achieve and establishing a clear vision

- What is the vision or goal?

- Why is this significant, valuable and worth our focus?

- What will guide us?

- What are our values?

- What's the plan?

- What will 'good' look like?

## Handling conflict, emotions and concerns

- What's the problem? What's behind that – what is *really* the problem?

- What would make this problem go away or reduce?

- What are your dominant emotions – how helpful are these?

- How can you reframe these emotions to be more helpful?

- What would you need to do or know for these concerns to reduce?

## Dealing with stress

- Remember, one person's stress is another person's normal, and with that in mind:

- What causes you stress – why is this? Is that normal?

- When do you typically become stressed – what triggers it? What are the circumstances?

- How do you behave when you are stressed?

- What is it like for those around you – what measures should you put in place for them, and for you?

- How well are you managing the stress of those around you?

- Do you anticipate and plan for stressful times?

- What measures could you put in place in advance to reduce stressful times (for yourself and others)?

- What actions could you take in the moment to reduce or banish stress (for yourself and others)?

## Developing boldness and audacious thinking

Becoming successfully audacious requires three elements: awareness, self-confidence and a compelling vision.

**Successfully audacious people have high levels of awareness** – in particular, self-awareness – that enables them to reflect and question what is going on. This insight allows them to recognize their own role in terms of their abilities and their impact on others. They are also aware of other people, objectively evaluating their strengths and weaknesses and judging what their likely responses and actions will be. Consider asking the coachee the following:

- How aware are you? Both in terms of self-awareness and more generally?

- How could you develop greater awareness – would that be useful?

- Are you picking up on faint signals as well as the obvious ones?

- How well – and how quickly – do you respond when something needs your attention?

- How could your responses improve?

**Building self-confidence and taking control** can be developed by recognizing that many situations, activities and opportunities possess a dangerous edge, a point at which we perceive that trauma may occur. To approach this point we need a protective frame, a way of viewing the situation so that we can deal with it. If such a frame exists, we can view the risk with excitement; without it, we are filled with anxiety. There are three levels of control needed to be audacious: control of the situation; control of contribution; control of reaction. The following questions should be useful as you coach your client towards building self-confidence and taking control:

- Where could you improve most, and where would it be most valuable: control of the situations you find yourself in; control of your contribution in those situations or control of your reaction?

- When do you lack confidence? How do you feel about this?

- What needs to change?

- Would it be useful if you were more confident in key situations and at key moments?

- What is holding you back? What are you afraid of?

- What sustained actions will you commit to taking to build confidence and control?

**Establishing a compelling vision and motivational connection** matters because it is motivationally rich, meaning that it appeals to a broad range of values in those who take part. Ask the coachee the following:

- Are you clear about your goal, values, the route to progress and success? Do you have a guiding vision?

- What's the plan – how will you make progress?

- What matters to you most?

Remember, when it comes to succeeding with tough questions and difficult situations, many of the tools, techniques and issues run in parallel – they are mutually supportive.

## CHAPTER 6

# Resilience and Emotion Questions

One of the most effective ways to coach someone to develop resilience is by focusing on four critical issues:

1. What they give their *attention* to – in particular, whether it is positive or negative

2. What they *think*

3. What practical *action* they take

4. What engages and *motivates* them when dealing with life's events.

Remember the words of Winston Churchill: 'Success is never final; failure is never fatal; the only thing that counts is courage.' Understanding and actively managing these issues makes a significant difference in someone's ability to manage life's challenges and pressures.

## Finding the best path through a tough place

Two other related points are crucial to remember when coaching and helping someone develop their resilience. First, the greatest stress is the stress we put on ourselves, and second, stress is personal for each individual. In other words, what worries, vexes or concerns me may not even be an issue for someone else.

To explore these points with your coachee, use the lines of questioning below.

### How much attention do you pay to negative and positive events?

- Why is this issue so important to you?

- Are you overemphasizing this one issue or event, or an aspect of this event?

- Would it help to change your area of focus, perhaps give attention to other issues?

- Do you have the right balance in your life – or are you overemphasizing certain things?

- Do you need to let go – or let go more? What would happen if you did?

- Looking back at the things that mattered to you when you were younger, is there anything you would want to tell your younger self?

### How do you think about positive and negative events?

- Do you spend enough time – meaning the right amount of time for *you* – coming to terms with negative events?

- What do you think when you encounter a negative (or specific type) of event?

- What do you think when something positive happens?

- How intentional is your thinking? How emotional is it?

- Do you tend to be overly positive or excessively negative when faced with issues or events?

- Looking back at past life events and your reaction to them, is there anything you would want to tell your younger self?

- How do you act – in particular, how do you deal with positive and negative events?

- How do you deal with positive events? How could this improve?

- What can you learn from the way you respond to positive news?

**How do you face something new or unfamiliar, or times of adversity?**

- Do you always act in the right way, at the right time?

- What do you typically do? How do you respond?

- How could you improve?

- Do you have a tendency to overemphasize one behaviour or another?

- How effective is your response usually? What would help you?

**What typically are your motivations when dealing with major events?**

- What are your values – what guides you?

- How is your self-awareness – what could improve, and what are your strengths?

- What are the thoughts, actions and motivations that are helping or hindering you?

- What gives you energy – and what takes your energy?

## Four questions to help develop resilience

The twenty-first century has presented us with a range of emotional moments, and at all levels: personally; professionally; for wider friends and family, and for society at large. Into this last category falls the usual excitement of sporting achievements, wider societal successes (e.g. massive reductions in global poverty, phenomenal innovations in technology) and also concerns (e.g. about global warming, political change). In addition, there are epoch-defining global moments that have the power to touch us profoundly: 9/11; the 2007–8 financial crisis; the COVID-19 pandemic – being the most obvious examples. Given the emotional rollercoaster ride that seems to characterize the times in which we live, it is little wonder that the desire to develop greater resilience has become particularly important. It is one of the fastest-growing areas of coaching: something that coaches worldwide are being asked to help with.

So, how do you help someone to develop greater resilience? A large part of the solution rests with the ability to help someone become adept at naming, handling and understanding their emotions and emotional triggers. The following four questions provide great jumping off points to help with this process, and other relevant questions then flow from these. The first two help an individual enhance their understanding; the last two help them find the best solution.

### 1 Are there *key events, people or situations* that you can examine and understand better?

The following questions are intended to explore the significance of events or situations:

- What happened? Or what do you think happened?

- Why did this happen?

- How did events unfold?

- Was it predictable?

- What forces led to this situation arising – what were the drivers of this event?

- What is the outcome or result – where are we now?

- What meaning do you / did you assign to this event?

- What was the impact of this event – the consequences?

- How do you feel as a result?

- How do other people feel, and how do they view this event?

The following questions are intended to explore the significance of people and relationships:

- Tell me about this person – what are they like, what is their connection to you, and how do they make you feel?

- What would help you understand this person better?

- What would they say if they knew they made you feel like this?

- When is this person at their best?

- When is this person not at their best?

- Is it possible that you are partly responsible for their reaction to you? Is your behaviour prompting an undesirable response?

- What can you do to improve your responses and feelings? Specifically, are there any mindset shifts and changes in understanding that you could make that would help, how does this person need to change?

- How could the relationship with this person improve – how can you make this happen?

## 2 Are you experiencing a build-up of emotion? Would it help to understand these emotions better?

- When are you most emotional?

- What triggers your emotions?

- How do you handle emotions?

- Which emotions are your strengths?

- Which emotions tend to typically present you with challenges?

- Thinking about your dominant emotions – how are these typically expressed by you, and how are they experienced by others?

## 3 Is there sufficient *compassion* – are you being reasonable and kind to yourself and others?

- Do you focus enough on yourself – your health and welfare?

- Are you kind to yourself, or are you tough on yourself?

- How compassionate are you? What evidence do you have of your compassion and kindness?

- Could you increase your compassion?

- Do you *show* empathy – understanding for how someone else thinks and feels?

- Is it possible that while you feel empathy and compassion, you could do more to show it?

- Are you overly compassionate – is it a strength that can sometimes become overplayed? What evidence do you have for this?

- Do you show gratitude – if so, how, and how often? Could this improve?

**4 What gives you energy? What would be better issues for you to focus on?**

- When do you feel most energized?

- When do you feel least energized?

- What mindset do you have, and what situations are you in when you feel energized?

- What, specifically, are you doing, and what is it about what you're doing, that brings enjoyment and energy?

- What changes can you make – possibly in your routine, situation, relationships, work or something else – to increase and enhance your energy?

- Do you have a go-to activity that increases your energy? (For many people this would involve exercise, or speaking with a loved one, for example.)

## Helping someone manage their emotions

There is a strong correlation between being aware of one's emotions and handling them effectively, and achieving happiness, fulfilment and success. Proving this point is the converse: mishandling one's emotions results in unhappiness, frustration and disappointment. It is important to recognize, however, that emotions are a good thing – they need to be because they are here to stay! In a revealing study by Alan S.

Cowen and Dacher Keltner of the University of California, Berkeley, 27 distinct categories of emotions were identified. They are listed alphabetically below, and while debate about the range of emotions varies widely, this list provides a useful practical starting point. As you review this list, you might want to take a moment and ask:

• What are the dominant emotions for me?

• What are the dominant emotions for the people I coach (including team members)?

It is often said that what matters most about emotions is not simply the emotion, *but what we choose to do with it*. So, which emotions do you need to express more or better? Here's the list:

| | | |
|---|---|---|
| • Admiration | • Confusion | • Interest |
| • Adoration | • Craving | • Joy |
| • Aesthetic appreciation | • Disgust | • Nostalgia |
| | • Empathetic pain | • Romance |
| • Amusement | • Entrancement | • Sadness |
| • Anxiety | | |
| | • Envy | • Satisfaction |
| • Awe | | |
| | • Excitement | • Sexual desire |
| • Awkwardness | • Fear | • Sympathy |
| • Boredom | | |
| | • Horror | • Triumph |
| • Calmness | | |

I believe that the issue of effectively handling emotions goes a long way to determining an individual's success or failure. Almost all of the successful people I can think of are emotional, and, crucially, they handle their emotions well. This includes great political leaders (Nelson Mandela, Angela Merkel, Barack Obama), sports coaches (Mike Krzyzewski ('Coach K'), Jill Ellis, José Mourinho), business leaders, innovators, philanthropists (Indra Nooyi, Jeff Bezos, Anne Sweeney, Bill Gates, Warren Buffett, Elon Musk, Jack Ma). Of course, these people have achieved much and are often exceptional, possibly weird, definitely 'special' and with emotions that may range widely, but they are never (or at least never appear to be) emotional wrecks, or *excessively* emotional. To the casual observer, at least, these vastly different and successful people all share the ability to display and channel their emotions appropriately, authentically and effectively, perhaps with the very occasional human lapse or idiosyncrasy.

These success stories can be contrasted with people that I regard as less successful. It is perhaps unfair to list here the people that I think are in this category, but there is one well-known person who is often regarded as being overly emotional, and whose emotions went a long way to undermining his popularity, reputation and effectiveness: former US President Donald Trump. It is not simply that he appeared to be inappropriately emotional; much more significant was his marked inability to handle his emotions positively.

All of this points to two significant insights that are relevant for all of us, both of which can be framed as questions.

1. Given that emotions are so ubiquitous and important, **how resilient are you?** By that I mean how effectively do you navigate your emotions, sailing through the turbulent or unfamiliar to reach equilibrium on the other side?

2. **What strengths do you have that can be overplayed?** In overplaying your strengths are they becoming a weakness, a source of vulnerability leading to a range of unintended consequences? (This is one question that could certainly have been asked of Donald Trump.)

It is valuable when coaching someone to help them build a greater understanding of their emotions. In much of society and business, in particular, we are not practised or, frankly, good enough at considering and exploring emotional issues. When it comes to emotions, we show them to our children, but only occasionally or haphazardly do we teach them about emotions. When circumstances, parenting, personalities and other factors align, we produce emotionally adept members of society, and when something goes wrong (e.g. a war or global pandemic, or perhaps a personal tragedy) our societies are left with otherwise capable, brave, normal people who are afflicted with emotional scars, something that they then often pass on to subsequent generations. For these reasons, the time for helping people to understand and manage their emotions is overdue: it is something we all need to get much, much better at, and it is rightly one of the most significant aspects of professional coaching.

## Questions to build emotional awareness, insight and understanding

Several of the categories of emotions highlighted by Cowen and Keltner provide a useful starting point for a deeper coaching conversation, enabling people to better understand the nature and implications of their emotions. If it seems to you or your coachee that they would benefit from greater understanding of emotions in general – or one or two in particular – then that could be a good place to start. This list does not cover all the emotions listed above – there are simply too many to cover effectively – but instead we consider some of the more frequent, relevant or significant emotions.

### Admiration and adoration

- Who do you admire most, and why?

- Who should you admire more, but don't? Why is that?

- Who, currently, are your role models – the people who operate in a way that can provide insights or guidance for you?

- What qualities do your role models possess that you could also develop? What can you learn from them?

- How open are you to other people? How well do you assess and understand the behaviour and emotions of others? Could this vital skill be improved? How?

- How much do you learn from other people that helps you in your work and life? How well do you learn from them?

- Where can you find useful role models?

- Is admiration an alien concept to you, something with which you are unfamiliar or uncomfortable? Why is that?

- What achievements are most impressive to you?

- How and when do you tell people how you feel about them?

- Do you share feelings of adoration, respect and esteem enough?

- Do you feel like you are held in high regard? If so, by whom?

- What is it about you that sparks a deep emotional connection and feelings of respect?

- What personal qualities, people or behaviours give you energy?

- What would you like to be your epitaph?

- What do you like and dislike about yourself?

- What do other people like and admire about you?

**Aesthetic appreciation**

- What moves you?

- What impresses you?

- What do your personal likes and dislikes tell you about yourself?

- Do you have the right amount of aesthetic appreciation in your life?

**Amusement**

- What makes you smile?

- How do you relax? Is this enough? If you do not relax enough, how could this improve?

- Do you take things too seriously, or not seriously enough?

- Would it help yourself or others to relax a little more?

- Do you laugh when you shouldn't? Humour, closely related to amusement, can be a strength that is sometimes overplayed; so, are you excessively or inappropriately amused?

- How well do you engage, enthral or inspire other people? Could this improve?

**Anxiety and fear**

- What situations, people or triggers typically cause you stress or anxiety?

- How do you feel when you are stressed – what do you do to resolve or improve the situation?

- What more can you do to prepare for times of anxiety or fear?

- Looking back, what would help you feel less anxious or fearful about a situation?

- Can you do more to avoid situations of anxiety or fear?

- Why (*not* when) do you feel fear? Is it reasonable and well-founded?

- What qualities could you develop, including skills and mindset shifts, that would help you in times of anxiety or fear?

## Awe

- What impresses you?

- Are you sufficiently open to seeing things that are positive? These matter because they can help us learn, relax, engage our range of emotions, or simply feel better.

## Awkwardness

- When are you least comfortable? How does this manifest – and why?

- What embarrasses you, and what makes you feel uncomfortable? Why?

- What can you do about this and what would help you: a) to prepare, and b) feel better in the moment?

## Boredom

- What issues, situations and behaviours bore you?

- How easily do you maintain focus on things that matter? How could this improve?

## Calmness

- Are you sufficiently calm? When are you not calm, and why?

- What more can you do to become calmer (either in general, or at specific times)?

- Are you too calm?

- Do you show sufficient emotion?

- What is your impact on others?

## Confusion

- When – and why – do you get confused, and why is this emotion significant for you?

- What do you wish you understood better?

- What do you need to know or learn – and how will you develop this insight?

## Craving

- What do you like? What do you need?

- What makes you feel better?

- What are your addictions – do these need to change?

- What drives you?

## Disgust

- What disappoints or appals you?

- What behaviours or situations that you encounter leave you feeling disgusted?

- What shocks you?

## Empathetic pain and sympathy

- How easy is it for you to walk in someone else's shoes? Do you do this too much, or not enough?

- Do you always show the right level of empathy at the right time, in the right way?

- Who do you care for? Do they know that you care for them?

## Excitement, entrancement and interest

- What thrills you?

- Do you have enough, too much or too little excitement in your life? What changes would you like to make, ideally?

- What interests you? Are you sufficiently able to follow your interests – could you do this more?

- Can you build on those things that fascinate, interest or excite you?

## Fear and horror

- What concerns do you have?

- What situations cause you stress?

- When have you been most stressed or fearful? How did you come through it?

- Have past events or traumas left you with lasting fears? Would counselling be useful?

## Joy

- When are you happiest?

- When do you experience 'flow' – a feeling that you are at the top of your game? How can you build on this feeling?

## Nostalgia

- What can you learn from the past (your past)?

- What have been the most powerful influences on your life? How have these influences shaped you?

- What would you like to do or find again?

- Draw your *river of life* – the events and the journey you have taken during your life, the things that shaped you, and then answer the following questions:
  - What do you take pride in?
  - What gives you strength?
  - What would you avoid, and repeat?
  - What are the lessons? What can you learn about yourself?

## And finally...

- What makes you feel:
  - sad?
  - satisfied?
  - pleased?

- What can you do to build on these emotions?

- What can you learn from them?

- How can you increase their frequency and intensity? What changes do you need to make?

- What will it feel like to experience these emotions?

One of the most important issues when handling emotions is to avoid straying out of the role of a professional coach. Remember that there are times when another type of intervention – for example, counselling – may be more appropriate.

# CHAPTER 7

# Decision-Making and Problem-Solving Questions

Decision-making is the essence of leadership, and the ability to consistently make the best decisions remains one of the defining skills of a leader in any situation. Crucially, the impact of our decisions can be influenced by environmental factors, risk, uncertainty and good and bad luck – all things outside of our control.

The focus in this chapter is on self-coaching, but the questions it contains work just as well when coaching others.

## Five big questions to help develop your decision-making style

There are certain things we can do to raise the quality of our process and ensure that our decision-making will tend to reflect a better, more consistent and strategic approach that delivers long-term benefits.

### 1 Are you going to solve the right problems with your decision-making?

In other words, are you making a decision that will tackle the root cause of a problem, or merely alleviate its symptoms?

In a business context it might be a more sensible use of time and resource to make the decisions that can solve systemic failings, rather than constantly acting to plug gaps and fix mistakes arising from them.

Other key questions at this stage include:

- What is the core issue you need to resolve?

- What are the implications (potential consequences) of this issue or decision?

- What related issues also need resolving, but at another time or in another way?

- What lessons are to be learned? How did we arrive in this situation, and what are the immediate implications that we may also need to address?

- Do you have enough information or resources to tackle this issue – would it be better or worse to wait?

## 2 Are you framing your decision-making in the most appropriate way?

Looking at the possible outcomes of a decision from only one perspective may blind you to other equally important and possible outcomes. Look at a problem from a regulator's, a competitor's or a customer's point of view to see a broader context. Be willing to re-examine your understanding of a decision and its possible repercussions to appreciate how it will impact others. Always consider a range of perspectives to give proper balance and judgement to your deliberations.

To help with this, author Steven Johnson recommends using decision maps to lay out a series of choices and options for the most important choices you make. These 'influence diagrams' could help you see the 'chain of effects' of your potential choices much more clearly. To enable yourself to build an accurate map, Johnson urges you to identify the issue or problem accurately and to get multiple perspectives.

Turning to you, the decision-maker, and your team:

- Can you reframe the problem or issue in a more positive or productive way?

- What would 'good' look like?

- What is the vision for your solution – the ideal outcome?

- How will you know when it's been resolved?

- Is the team equipped and ready to solve the problem?

- Who needs to know about the issue, and whose support is required?

## 3 Are you making the right assumptions?

Every decision is based on certain assumptions, but are those assumptions justified? There are three ways we should consider the reliability of what we assume to be the case before we act:

- What do we know and recognize?

- What data do we have available? What data do we need, and how (or where) will we get it?

- What is unknown and unfamiliar? How do we fill the gaps in our understanding?

- What do we know but can't prove?

- What do we know but haven't questioned?

- What can we know for sure and what are the gaps we are filling in for ourselves?

- Listing the extent and limits of our current knowledge can be a good exercise in judging our ability to make the right call.

We don't really like to admit what we don't know. Leaders and charismatic people will often tell stories to fill in the knowledge gaps, which can rapidly become a new and dangerous 'fact' based on nothing but supposition and a fear of saying 'I don't know'.

The Johari Window is a valuable, popular and effective technique for assessing the level of understanding and data behind a situation requiring a decision. To use the technique, take time (either individually as a coach or together with your coachee) to, first, reflect on the critical elements in each quadrant, and second, focus in on the most significant quadrant, the issues involved and their implications for your decision.

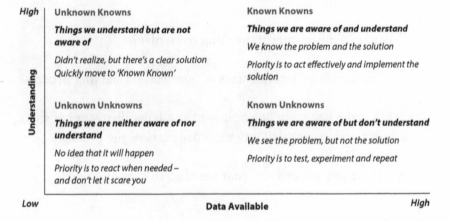

| High | Unknown Knowns | Known Knowns |
|---|---|---|
| | *Things we understand but are not aware of* | *Things we are aware of and understand* |
| | Didn't realize, but there's a clear solution Quickly move to 'Known Known' | We know the problem and the solution Priority is to act effectively and implement the solution |
| **Understanding** | Unknown Unknowns | Known Unknowns |
| | *Things we are neither aware of nor understand* | *Things we are aware of but don't understand* |
| | No idea that it will happen Priority is to react when needed – and don't let it scare you | We see the problem, but not the solution Priority is to test, experiment and repeat |
| Low | Data Available | High |

The Johari Window

## 4 Methodology – are you balancing intuition with data?

The way in which we intend to solve a problem is the bit of decision-making that is usually neglected, but it can have a huge impact on outcomes. You should ensure that the implementation of a decision is not hampered by lack of buy-in or understanding by the people who will need to enact it.

A simple process for decision-making includes several elements:

## Assessing the situation

- What are the key issues or principles here? What needs resolving, and why?

- Is this important, or urgent, or both?

- When does the situation need resolving – what is our timeframe?

- Who is currently involved or affected, and who do we need to include or inform?

## Defining the critical issues

- What is the most important thing to resolve?

- Are there critical dependencies in our decision-making process?

- What is the key – the lynchpin – to resolving this issue? Is there a single action that will unlock other parts of the process?

- Are there any sensitivities that we need to keep in mind?

## Specifying the decision

- Sometimes the process and implementation is as important as – or more important than – the decision itself, so how do we need to implement the solution?

- If multiple issues need resolving, what are the priorities?

- What are the obstacles to the ideal solution? What do you need to make it happen – and how can you achieve this?

## Making the decision

- What are our options?

- What is not optional – what are the essentials?

- Ideally, what would be the best solution?

- Who have you involved in making the decision – is there anyone else you can ask or involve?

Is this decision similar to anything else? Are there lessons you can apply from elsewhere?

## Implementing the decision

- Who do you need to involve and inform?

- Whose help and support do you need to implement the decision? How will you get this?

- Sometimes the process and implementation is as important as the decision itself, so how should the decision be implemented? How should the problem be solved?

- What are the potential pitfalls and risks?

- How can inherent risks be managed and mitigated?

- Are you in the right frame of mind to address the issue? If not, why, and how, can you prepare and improve your mindset?

- Are there parts of the decision that you can delay?

Monitoring the decision and making adjustments as events unfold

- Are there any milestones or key indicators that you should monitor as you implement the decision?

- How will you know if the decision/solution is successful?

- Are there key performance indicators you need to monitor?

- Would it be useful for a group to monitor the decision and act as events unfold?

- How will you communicate, and with whom?

Throughout this process you should be checking with others, communicating, avoiding biases and using your intuition.

It may help to reflect on a recent significant decision and consider where you could have improved your approach.

### 5 Reflect on experience – is there a precedent or a lesson to be learned?

We shouldn't assume that there is no precedent for the business choices we face. It's worth considering how different leaders in the near or even distant past have approached the kind of problems that we are trying to solve right now.

- Are there examples of this decision being resolved from elsewhere? How did it work?

- Have you conducted an after action review (AAR) (see Chapter 14)?

- Who should be involved in a review of the decision?

- How will you learn from the decision?

- What are the lessons and implications for the future?

## Avoiding pitfalls and decision-making biases

Bad decisions can often be traced back to the way the decisions were made: the alternatives were not clearly defined; the right information was not collected; the costs and benefits were not accurately weighed. However, sometimes the fault lies not in the decision-making process, but in the mind of the decision-maker: the way that the human brain works can sabotage the choices we make.

In a 1998 *Harvard Business Review* paper, John S. Hammond, Ralph L. Keeney and Howard Raiffa highlighted several psychological traps that are particularly likely to affect the way that business decisions are made. Which of these might you be most vulnerable to?

### The anchoring trap

This trap leads us to give disproportionate weight to the first information that we receive. This often happens because of the initial impact of the first information and our immediate reaction to it.

- Are you or your colleagues at risk of giving disproportionate weight to the first piece of information you receive?

- Can you think of examples when this may have happened to you or someone else?

- How prone are you to falling into this trap, on a scale from 1 (highly unlikely) to 10 (very likely – I do it all the time)?

- What measures can you put in place to avoid it happening? What would work best for you?

- The antidote is to be sure about what is happening and waiting as long as possible, to ensure that you have all the information – and possibly some different options, too. Are you doing this?

## The status quo trap

The status quo trap biases us towards maintaining the current situation – even when better alternatives exist. This might be caused by inertia or by the potential loss of face if the current position was to change.

- Are you wary of changing course, potentially at risk of sticking with the wrong course for too long? If so, why?

- How can you overcome a reluctance to change?

- What, exactly, are the risks of staying the course for too long?

- What are the risks of trying a different approach – and how can these risks be reduced?

- The best solutions to the status quo trap are openness, honesty and courage – do you have enough of these qualities? How could you improve your openness, honesty and ability to try the unknown or do something courageous?

- Can you think of examples when this may have happened to you or someone else?

- How prone are you to falling into this trap, on a scale from 1 (highly unlikely) to 10 (very likely – I do it all the time)?

- What measures can you put in place to avoid it happening? What would work best for you?

## The sunk-cost trap

This trap inclines us to perpetuate the mistakes of the past, on the grounds that 'we have invested so much in this approach/decision that we cannot abandon it or alter course now'. The management accountant's view of this is refreshing: if it's spent, it's spent – worry about the present and future, not the past.

- What is stopping you from changing course at the right time? What would help you?

- Can you think of examples when this may have happened to you or someone else?

- How prone are you to falling into this trap, on a scale from 1 (highly unlikely) to 10 (very likely – I do it all the time)?

- What measures can you put in place to avoid it happening? What would work best for you?

## The confirming-evidence trap

The confirming-evidence trap results in us seeking out information to support an existing predilection and to discount opposing information.

- Do you look for evidence to justify a decision rather than comprehensively reviewing the decision?

- How do you typically respond when you receive information that undermines a decision you made?

- How open and approachable are you? Can people share bad news with you readily? Is this something you can improve?

- Does information and knowledge flow easily and readily to the places where it's needed? Is it requested, updated, comprehensive, relevant and valued?

- Can you think of examples when the confirming-evidence trap may have happened to you or someone else?

- What measures can you put in place to avoid it happening? What would work best for you?

### The framing trap

The framing trap occurs when we incorrectly state a problem, totally undermining the decision-making process. This is often unintentional, but not always.

- Do you take sufficient care when framing a problem or decision?

- Do you look at how you could reframe decisions? Do you ask for help framing (and reframing) decisions?

- Can you think of examples when the framing trap may have caused difficulties?

- What measures can you put in place to avoid it happening? What would work best for you?

### The overconfidence trap

This common pitfall makes us overestimate the accuracy of our forecasts.

- Are you overconfident? What makes you certain of your answer?

- We can all be overconfident at certain times: when are you potentially overconfident?

- Can you think of times when the overconfidence trap may have caused difficulties?

- What measures can you put in place to avoid it happening? What would work best for you?

- Is there a single specific element of your decision-making that is potentially overconfident – for example, your faith in a colleague or in a piece of information?

## The prudence trap

The prudence trap leads us to be overcautious when we make estimates about uncertain factors.

- How prone are you to falling into this trap, on a scale from 1 (highly unlikely) to 10 (very likely – I do it all the time)?

- We can all be overcautious at certain times: when are you most vulnerable (most cautious)?

- Can you think of times when the prudence trap may have caused difficulties?

- What measures can you put in place to avoid it happening? What would work best for you?

- Is some level of prudence beneficial? Remember, prudence is fine; it is excessive caution that can be problematic. Remember, it is *excessive* caution that is the problem.

- Realism, perhaps erring on the side of caution (depending on the nature of the decision), is the antidote to overconfidence and prudence. How realistic are you? How can you enhance your realism?

## The recent event trap

This trap leads us to give undue weight to a recent and, quite probably, dramatic event (or sequence of events). This is very similar to the anchoring trap, except that it can arise at any time, not just at the start, and cause a misjudgement.

- Awareness of the trap and your susceptibility to it (for example, whether you are typically excessively cautious or confident about decisions) is vital for avoiding it. How prone are you to falling into this trap, on a scale from 1 (highly unlikely) to 10 (very likely – I do it all the time)?

- Can you think of times when the recent event trap may have caused difficulties?

- What measures can you put in place to avoid it happening – what would work best for you?

## Bolstering – an uncritical emphasis on one option

The bolstering trap tends to happen when there is no 'good' option available, only a choice among the 'least worst' courses of action. Bolstering is a way of coping with difficult choices and it can result in a sense of invulnerability to external events, especially when it is accompanied by an escalation of commitment (the sunk-cost trap).

- Are you choosing between 'least good' options – if so, is this sufficiently understood, or are people wasting their time looking for the impossible?

- Bolstering can result in poor contingency planning in the event that the favoured option falters or fails. So, how good is your contingency planning?

- Are you reconciled with the decision and sufficiently committed to making it work? This can be difficult if there are problems inherent in the solution, but it still may be the best way forward.

## Shifting responsibility

This trap is another way of coping with difficult decisions and is often a sign of weak leadership. Usually, because of a decision dilemma, a decision-maker will pass responsibility for the choice to another person or group.

- The big problem with shifting responsibility is that this will create a climate of fear and blame. Are you at risk of inappropriately and unhelpfully blaming others when something goes wrong?

- How well do you cope with making difficult decisions?

- How well do you respond when decisions go right – and when they go wrong?

## Cultural flaws: fragmentation and groupthink

Cultural flaws can hinder effective strategic decision-making in two opposite ways: fragmentation and groupthink.

*Fragmentation* occurs when people are in disagreement. Dissent often festers in the background – for example, in mutterings among colleagues – rather than raised openly.

*Groupthink* is when an impression of harmonious agreement is given because ideas that do not support the line a group is taking are suppressed. It may occur because individuals are denied information or lack the confidence or ability to challenge the dominant views of the group. Close-knit groups also tend to rationalize the invulnerability of their decisions, inhibiting analysis.

- Are you vulnerable to fragmentation or groupthink? If so, when? What is the solution?

- Do you actively seek out diverse opinions when making decisions – insights from people who are markedly different (and possess significantly different experience) from you?

- Are you concerned about division, argument or dissent when making decisions? Could this lead to groupthink – going along with the view of the majority? (If you think you may be susceptible to groupthink then it may help to watch the classic 1957 film *12 Angry Men*, a courtroom drama directed by Sidney Lumet.)

## World-class decision-making: putting it into practice

Two common mistakes beset decision-making. The first is to react to a situation as if it were a unique series of events, when the problem it reflects is a generic one requiring the application of a consistent rule, principle or strategy. This results from an inability to see the big picture or to understand where the events might lead.

- Do you make enough use of information and data when solving problems or making decisions?

- How well does key information (potential warning signs that there may be a problem developing) flow to the right people at the right time?

- How could you improve your contingency planning? Is that potentially a problem?

- How prepared are you to respond to grey rhinoceros events (high-probability, high-impact, yet neglected threats) or black swan events (low-probability, high-impact events)? From an economic recession to a pandemic, natural disaster or terrorist attack, are you and your colleagues fully prepared in terms of resources and mindset? What more could you do?

- Where are you most vulnerable when it comes to the decision-making or problem-solving process? Along the path from first realizing there's a problem to finally achieving a successful outcome, where could you improve?

- How could: a) your team, and b) your organization improve its decision-making capability?

- Do you consistently apply common principles, values and perhaps even a guiding vision when making decisions?

- One mistake is to perceive a situation as if it were a generic issue requiring an old solution; if it is a new type of situation, then a new solution is required.

- How creative and innovative are you when solving problems or making decisions?

- Are you sufficiently bold, or overly cautious, in your decision-making style?

- Do you learn well enough from your decisions?

- Do you conduct after action reviews?

- Do you do enough to invite and provide feedback when making and implementing decisions?

- The outcome is, of course, usually the most important thing when making decisions – but it is rarely the *only* thing to keep in mind. Are you at risk of focusing on outcomes at the expense of other issues (e.g. achieving other objectives, maintaining team-work, retaining talent)?

- Would it help to start with a meta-decision: decide the way you are going to decide?

- Do you make enough use of your experience and good judgement?

- Are you sufficiently confident when making decisions? When do you lack confidence, and how can you build decision-making confidence and capability?

Decisions are a vital aspect of leadership and they feature prominently when coaching – helping someone find the best way forward is a vital and defining role of a coach. Despite its significance, however, we rarely focus on our decision-making style, and our strengths and weaknesses in this area. For this reason, a coach has a vital role to play: enabling individuals to be more intentional and aware in the choices they make.

## CHAPTER 8

# Questions on Purpose

Understanding and explicitly recognizing life goals, aspirations and priorities is valuable, both for individuals and the organizations they work for. However, crucially, employees need to create a *personal purpose* that not only aligns with the organization but also correlates to their particular context. For individuals, a personal purpose helps to highlight how executives should use their time and energy to accomplish what they need to do. It provides clarity, and fuels the courage that is sometimes needed in order to dig into issues, even if it is difficult. Remember, it is purpose that provides the focus, encouragement and drive needed to succeed.

### Helping someone find their personal purpose and goal

With that in mind, there are several pillars that will support someone's life's purpose. Focusing on these will enable you to coach someone (including yourself) to find and succeed with their purpose.

- **Self-awareness:** Helping someone understand and benefit from their life's purpose requires a deep understanding of themselves and how they currently live their life.

- **Personal motivations:** Helping someone unlock their life's purpose requires understanding of the internal motivations that drive their behaviour.

- **Life experience:** When finding personal purpose it is valuable to help someone process and understand their experience.

- **Aspirations and dreams:** This key to unlocking life's purpose involves helping someone tune into their deepest and most profound aspirations for the future.

- **Creating an ideal:** Closely linked with dreams, this aspect of helping someone unlock their life's purpose requires organization and planning, enabling the individual to envision their ideal life.

- **Higher calling:** To ensure that the person's purpose is meaningful and sustainable, it is important to help your coachee tune into the deepest parts of their psyche, so they can use it to give meaning to their life and work.

The following questions will help you to challenge and guide someone who is keen to develop their personal purpose. It will focus their thinking on themselves, their life and their circumstances.

## Self-awareness and purpose questions

These questions are designed to help you support and coach someone so they gather deeper insights about their personality, roles, strengths, weaknesses, and about how they are perceived by others.

- What do you feel you are meant to do in the world?

- Where have you found real satisfaction and a sense of purpose?

- What did you want to be when you were a child?

- Which attributes and aspects of your personality seem to stand out most?

- What are your talents and natural abilities?

- Where do your core strengths lie?

- Where are you most effective and productive?

- What are your three most significant weaknesses?

- What do you find most challenging? Where do you struggle most?

- What kind of activities and roles do you enjoy?

- Which roles do you feel are best suited to your core strengths?

- What life roles just don't suit you?

- How would your close friends and family describe what you are like? What would you think of their description?

- What do others think you are meant to do (or most suited to do) with your life?

- What is your family's background, impact and legacy?

- What do you think of this legacy, and what part do you want to play?

- What part does family play in your future?

These questions will begin to provide a clear overview of an individual's strengths, interests and weaknesses. Typically – but not always – our life's purpose is found in our strengths and interests. It is also possible that one's purpose could emerge as a result of fears and challenges coming to light.

## Personal motivations and purpose

A vital part of understanding one's purpose is to develop a deep awareness of motivations, passions and areas of greatest fulfilment. The questions below will help an individual coachee to better understand their internal motivations and the drivers behind their behaviour.

- What are your passions?

- Who inspires you?

- Where do you find most inspiration?

- What would you struggle to let go?

- What causes are you most passionate about?

- If you had only one year to live, what would you focus on?

- What three things do you most look forward to doing?

- What three things do you most dislike doing?

- What's been the most satisfying thing you have ever done?

- What have you accomplished that you are most proud of?

- What have you done that you would like to do again or more often?

- What activities make you feel excited, energized and invigorated?

## Life experience questions

Our experiences shape who we are today. Typically, our life purpose becomes clearer when we review the experiences that have helped shape who we are. Crucially, it is our experiences, dreams, desires, aspirations, motivations and personal insights about who we are and what gives us energy that helps us recognize and uncover our life's purpose. The questions below will help you to explore the coachee's life experience and purpose.

• What valuable knowledge and skills have you gained at work?

• How is your work and career path intertwined with your destiny?

• What have been your greatest career accomplishments?

• How do you tend to help others who need your assistance?

• What key skills have you picked up that are of most value to you?

• What unique abilities do you have that separate you from others?

• What have all your failures prepared you for?

• How have all your failures been of value? What insights have you gained from them?

• What have all your experiences over a lifetime prepared you for?

• What specific life experiences have had the most meaning?

- What life experiences have shaped your personality and character in the most profound way?

- How can you draw on these experiences to live a happier and more fulfilling life?

- How could you use these experiences to help you accomplish your dreams and aspirations?

## The fuel of personal purpose: dreams and aspiration questions

- The key to unlocking someone's life's purpose also involves helping them tune into their most heartfelt, significant and profound aspirations for the future.

- What would you like to do with your life?

- What would you do if you could not fail?

- What dreams would you pursue if you had unlimited potential?

- What specifically would you like to experience?

- What things would you like to learn?

- What types of skills would you like to master?

- How would you like to express your creativity?

- What things would you like to create?

- What would you regret most not doing?

- What would you regret most if you simply played it safe?

## Questions for creating the ideal life

Closely linked with dreams is the notion of helping someone come to understand and envision their ideal life. This will help them find the fuel and drive to move them forwards, towards this goal.

The following questions will help you guide someone to build an ideal life and career path. While working through these questions it is important to help them take into account all of the answers they have already provided and, where relevant, go back and adjust these.

It is vital to remember that this is about building an *ideal* picture or vision of one's life. It is important, therefore, to make it as bold, personal, engaging, inspiring, meaningfuland detailed as possible.

- What would your ideal life look like?

- What would your ideal lifestyle be like?

- What would your ideal day look like from morning till night? Describe it in detail.

- What would be your ideal week, month and year be like? Describe it in detail.

- Given your passions, experience and abilities, what career path would be an ideal fit?

- What is your ideal job description? Write it down in detail.

- What does your ideal weekly work schedule look like? Describe it in detail.

Answering these questions should now give you more clarity about what an ideal future might look like. Although this is still a hypothetical future that doesn't require any planning or realism, it is, nonetheless, a potential future based on the answers to the questions above. This future is therefore built on your greatest passions, interests, strengths, dreams and the incredible experiences you have had over a lifetime that have shaped your character.

## Higher-calling questions

The preceding questions, designed to help someone find their future, should have resonated at a profoundly deep level. Now all that's left is to tie all this together to discover their higher calling.

There is psychological evidence that we are never truly fulfilled unless we are working on something greater than ourselves for the benefit of others. This, of course, doesn't mean that you need to do something that changes the world. What it does mean is that we are only truly happy and fulfilled when focusing on something that makes a difference, in a big or small way.

The following is a list of questions that will help you to unlock your own or your coachee's spiritual purpose and higher calling through service to others.

- What kind of people do you/would you like to help?

- What types of issues do you care most about?

- Where could you provide most value to others?

- What individuals or groups do you most identify with?

- How have all your difficulties equipped you to serve others?

- What lasting legacy would you like to leave behind?

- How will the world be a better place because you have lived in it?

- What do you care about that is bigger than you?

- What problems would you like to solve?

- Given all this, what is your spiritual calling?

- Given what you know now, what is your one true life's purpose?

Having answered these questions, you or your coachee should now have a deeper and more profound understanding of what you/they could focus on in future that will help bring you/them more joy, happiness and fulfilment.

Crucially, it is important not to force or 'fake' these answers. The answers will come in time, and you may need to go through all these questions several times before you find the truest response, the one that sits best with you/your coachee. Most importantly of all, it's critical that you/your coachee take your first step into the unknown.

## Stepping into the future

Whether we have all the answers or not, it's vital that we take the first step, moving purposefully and intentionally in the right direction. At this point the following questions are pertinent:

- What will you do?

- What will you do first?

- What changes are you looking to make?

- What are your core values? What is guiding you?

- Are you listening to yourself well enough?

- Have you shared your vision and purpose with others?

- Are you ready for the inevitable setbacks? How will these be overcome?

Over time we will meet new people, experience new things, learn new skills, expose ourselves to new knowledge and information. We may also face setbacks and adversity that expose our weaknesses, strengthen our character and build emotional resilience. These are markers on our journey. They will help us find that one path; the one that makes us feel happy and contented, that leads us towards our life's purpose.

## Using personal purpose and goals to energize a business or team

The best way to revitalize a business while simultaneously energizing its people is to do several things purposefully. Tease this out by working through the following strands of questions.

### Create a shared culture of purpose

When a company engages people in developing a shared purpose, and then demonstrates a strong commitment to it, it becomes much easier for the company to be regarded as a force for good and a creator of value.

- What is our purpose?

- What do we believe in? What are our values?

- What aspects of our work are most valuable and meaningful?

### Think about the activities you could pursue that align with your purpose

These could be things that would both inspire employees and improve results.

- How do we – and how will we – put our purpose to work?

- What more could we do to reinforce our purpose?

- Is there anything we do that undermines our purpose?

**Ask for actions and support in emphasizing your purpose**

- Do you support our purpose? What aspect of our purpose resonates with you most?

- Do you have any objections or concerns?

- What will you do personally to support our purpose?

## Creating a shared culture of purpose

Explore how to create a shared culture of purpose by asking your coachee the following questions:

- Do you and your company communicate its purpose?

- Does everyone – and most especially people in leadership positions – demonstrate a strong commitment to the purpose?

- Do employees understand that the company genuinely aspires to be a force for good and a creator of value for all stakeholders, especially employees?

- What activities could you pursue that align with your purpose?

- What are the top three actions you could take that would both inspire employees and improve results?

- Have you asked colleagues for actions and support that emphasize your purpose?

## A quick, practical fix: finding purpose at work

If you or your coachee are looking to define their individual purpose, it helps to ask a series of questions:

- What are your personal aspirations and goals in your current role?

- What are your passions?

- What are your unique skills and abilities?

- What is most important to you?

- What are your dreams and aspirations?

- What do you want more time for, or to put energy into?

- What environments or settings feel the most natural to you?

- When, in work and life situations, are you most comfortable expressing your talents?

- What do you want for yourself?

The result is not (or is rarely) a crafted, wordy statement, something that is extrinsic to the individual. Instead, the outcome is intrinsic, *within* the individual, but has been discovered and made explicit. This outcome can then drive and guide the individual to develop, perform and succeed.

# PART 2

# Coaching Questions for Typical and Difficult Challenges

The following chapters focus on some of the most common coaching situations: helping someone succeed in a new role, for example, or enabling an individual to develop their leadership effectiveness. These chapters also address some of the toughest coaching challenges, including helping someone survive and thrive during times of transformation and change, communicate with impact and influence, work effectively across cultures, or simply refocus someone who has checked out, disengaged or lost their mojo.

These typical and difficult challenges are based on international research with a range of individual coaches and coaching organizations. However, there are at least three vital questions for every coach to consider. What do you find the most difficult coaching challenge? What, in your experience, are the issues that are most frequently presented? And, most importantly of all, how well equipped are you for the typical and difficult challenges that you face?

## CHAPTER 9

# Leadership and Teamwork Questions

At some point in their career a coach will work with a leader whose challenges, goals and priorities relate to leadership and teamworking. In this context several issues are especially significant: building and empowering the team; setting a clear direction; enabling people to succeed; and, once this is happening, building on their success. The questions in this chapter are intended to help coaches focus, support and challenge the leaders that they are working with.

## Developing a compelling vision, finding the right strategy or direction

A vision is a particularly useful aspect of objective setting because it helps provide people with guidance and a clear sense of direction. 'Vision' and 'visioning' can often be misunderstood, but the truth is that they simply mean developing a coherent description of the task or team in the future. A clear, dynamic vision provides a clear focus for action, guiding people's decisions at all levels and helping to instil both confidence and resolve. Also, visioning and visualization techniques can equally well be used at a personal level, to enable someone to get a clear focus on a personal-development or behavioural-change goal.

The following questions should help your coachee develop a compelling vision and clear sense of direction for their team:

- Do you have a clear, dynamic vision of the future that guides the way people work – what they know, do and believe?

- In what ways does the vision mobilize people and generate commitment?

- Does the vision provide a clear focus? If so, on what?

- Is the vision guided by a clear and explicit set of values?

- Does the vision promote confidence and support decision-making, problem solving and innovation?

- How effectively does the vision foster teamwork, consistency and alignment?

- Does the vision genuinely support people, and add or create value?

- Is the vision focused, specific and 'real-world' enough to be used as a basis for strategic planning and to guide decision-making?

- Is the vision adaptive, allowing for individual initiative in its attainment, and flexible enough to allow for changing conditions?

- How clearly expressed is the vision? For example, are there stories or examples that would help enhance understanding?

- Is the vision you are creating what you want – or are you at risk of simply accepting what other people believe? Have you done enough to decide for yourself what will be important in the future? (Your personal commitment and belief are essential.)

- Insights do not readily come from old information, so have you done enough to take account of trends and tried to understand why things are changing, not just how?

It is clearly essential for people in the team to understand and support the vision. With that in mind, ask the coachee:

- Are you communicating in an exciting and practical way?

- Are you speaking positively so that people are intrigued, challenged and motivated?

- Are you being honest and open, so that people trust you and the vision?

- Do you do enough to bring the vision to life, ideally with examples, and do you do this regularly?

- Do you encourage people to see what the vision means for their work?

## Assessing key aspects of personal leadership style

One point about leadership coaching is often misunderstood or neglected: the need to help someone find their own, genuine leadership style – an approach that is effective, comfortable, authentic and sustainable for the individual. Exploring this issue requires questions that are personal and, in some cultures, may even appear intrusive. It is important, therefore, that the coach's intent is clear: to help someone develop their personal leadership.

- What is your default leadership style? How would you describe your leadership?

- What is your preferred learning style?

- Do you put more faith in hard data (numbers and analyses) or soft data (expert assessments and others' opinions)? What are the implications of this approach – when is it a strength, and when is it a weakness?

- Do you prefer to learn by immersing yourself into a situation (an experiential learning style) or by observing for a while before taking action (a conceptual learning style)?

- What is your preferred communication style? Do you prefer that colleagues communicate in writing or in person?

- What is your motivational style?

- Do you tend to favour 'push' methods of motivating others, such as setting goals, measuring performance and offering incentives, or 'pull' methods, like creating a vision and inspiring teamwork?

- Do you change your approach to motivation in response to how individuals prefer to be motivated?

- What is your decision-making style?

- Do you prefer to make important decisions by consulting with subordinates and then making the call or by building consensus?

- To what extent do you flex your decision-making to suit the issues at hand?

- Compared with the typical manager at your level, do you tend to delegate more or less responsibility to subordinates?

- Overall, how does your leadership style fit with the culture of your organization?

## Delegating

How to delegate effectively, often in difficult or challenging circumstances (for example, as a new leader, or when working with a demanding colleague), is one of the most frequent challenges presented to coaches by the leaders they are working with. As a coach, what matters is getting to the heart of the issue for each individual – one size does not fit all – and there are several things that you can do when coaching, to help a leader explore and refine their approach in this area.

### 1 Preparing to delegate

- Are you a confident, relaxed delegator, or is it something you find difficult, or where you may lack experience? Which aspects of delegation could you improve?

- Do you have concerns or limiting beliefs when it comes to delegating? If so, what are they? How valid are they? How can they be best addressed and resolved?

- Are you focused on the outcome – the results that you want to be achieved?

- Do you have clear, precise objectives?

- Have you ensured careful consideration and planning, possibly discussions with other colleagues?

- You may also need to give some thought to priorities: what should come first?

- Have you considered both the importance and urgency of the task that you are delegating?

## 2 Matching person and task

- Are you choosing the right person? What makes them the right person?

- Does the person who is required to do the job understand it, and have the personal skills and competence to tackle it?

- Will the task stretch and challenge the individual?

- How much guidance or support will be needed from you?

- What, if any, are your concerns?

## 3 Discussing and agreeing objectives

- Have you discussed the task, from purpose to completion?

- Do you need to agree targets, objectives, resources, review points and deadlines?

- Do you need to check understanding and gain explicit agreement to your plan?

## 4 Providing resources and the appropriate level of authority

- Have you provided all the necessary resources?

- Does the individual have the authority to complete the task?

- Are roles, responsibilities and accountabilities clearly defined?

- Are you clear about how and when you will follow up?

## 5 Monitoring progress

Control does not mean interfering when there is no need, but it does mean checking progress at pre-planned and specified times. Control also involves verifying that things are on track. Monitoring and control ensures that the delegated task is completed successfully and that the desired results are achieved. The key to monitoring is to ensure that the person completing the task remains accountable.

- How will you monitor progress?

- Delegation without control is abdication – how much control will you retain, and how will you exert this control?

- Empowerment is a vital element of delegation – how empowered are the people working with you?

- Are you supporting and enabling the success of people around you? How could this be enhanced?


## 6 Reviewing and assessing overall performance

- Do you revise objectives, and check achievements against the agreed goals?

- Do you delegate with confidence and 'let go' of tasks you used to do?

- Do you let the person complete the task in the way they prefer?

- Do you view delegation as a way of developing skills, confidence and capability?

- Do you show trust, provide encouragement and instil belief?

- Are you prepared for the person completing the task to take risks, and are you supportive and constructive if mistakes are made?

- Are you sufficiently patient?

## Mastering empowerment

Empowerment is based on the belief that the full skills and capabilities of a team are frequently underused and that, given the right environment and level of responsibility, people will start to make a much greater, positive contribution. When empowering someone, a team leader is letting them get on with the job entirely: they are both responsible and accountable within certain agreed boundaries. To help your coachee master empowerment, ask the following questions:

- Are you comfortable and confident about letting each member of the team get on with their job? How could you improve this?

- Do you let those team members with the greatest insight and understanding take decisions themselves?

- Are you committed and effective at removing obstacles and unnecessary bureaucracy so that others can succeed?

- Do you do enough to encourage and enable people to put their ideas for improvement into practice? How could this improve?

- Do you set a clear, unambiguous direction and ensure that people remain on course?

- Are you able to retain a full understanding of what is happening?

- How well do you offer support, open doors and clear the way for action? Is it timely, and is this something you do without taking over?

- Do you empower others to make decisions, making only those decisions which others cannot, perhaps because they lack time, information or knowledge?

- Do you continuously assess performance, reward progress and support individual and team development?

- Do you build trust, and share information and knowledge, whenever possible?

- Do you do enough to let your colleagues and senior managers know your plans, and check that their expectations meet your own?

- Do you assess the barriers to empowerment? What are they (e.g., people may fear responsibility or there may be a culture of blame), and how can they be overcome?

- Do you build the right culture within your team?

- Are boundaries clearly established? Empowerment provides people with greater autonomy and responsibility, but it is vital to agree and set clear limits.

- Are you prepared to have boundaries tested?

- Could you do more to communicate and win support?

- Do those around you understand what is involved in empowerment? It may involve reassuring some, selling the benefits and winning the support of others.

- Do you make sure that people have the right skills and resources to take control?

- How often do you review what each member of your team does now, and what they are likely to be doing in future?

- Are objectives and performance measures clear and agreed? Empowerment is about giving people the responsibility and resources to complete tasks on an ongoing basis. As with delegation, it is not about dumping work on people and leaving them, and it requires you to agree the necessary level of speed, accuracy and cost-efficiency.

## Developing a personal elevator pitch

An elevator pitch is a brief (20–30-second) overview of an individual created by them to say who they are and what they do as a way of introducing themselves to colleagues and new contacts. Imagine you're standing in an elevator and a senior colleague arrives in the lift, presses the button and introduces themselves. How would you reply? What would you say? You can get the coachee to do something similar.

The great thing about an elevator pitch is that we have time to think it through and prepare. It doesn't need to take long to devise one: after all, everyone is an expert on themselves! The following questions will help your coachee develop a pitch.

- Are you clear about what is important to you? Your values, priorities and strengths – who you are?

- Can you describe something positive or different at the heart of what you do?

- How easily, and how often, do you show your passion? Are you avoiding the temptation to simply be flat or descriptive (e.g. 'What I really enjoy about it is...' or 'One of the great things about my job is...').

- Would it be useful to give further examples or information?

- Are you genuinely, authentically yourself? Would it be useful to imagine that you're talking to an interested friend or family member, or yourself at a different moment in time?

- Is your elevator pitch up to date? Can you include recent stories or examples? (e.g. 'At the moment I'm...' or 'There was a great example recently when I...').

- Is your elevator pitch – your description of you – sufficiently personalized, engaging, and adaptable for different groups?

- Do you have a couple of open questions that you can ask – for example, 'What do you think about...?' and then refer to an interesting recent development or common interest?

- Do you have a format and style that feels comfortable and suits your personality?

### Elevating team performance

There are several important questions a team leader should keep in mind when elevating team performance, as well as practical actions they can take. Ask your coachee the following to make sure they have internalized these questions or are beginning to do so.

- Are you focusing sufficiently on team development?

Research shows that employees typically have a greater affinity with their team than with the broader organization. This is especially true for younger employees (under 35). Therefore, developing teams can have the benefit of increasing the chance of engaging and retaining high potentials.

- Do you have a team development plan?

- Does your team have:
  - *a team charter* – a guide to how team members will interact and behave (e.g. maintain collective cabinet responsibility, meet deadlines, etc.)?
  - *a guiding vision* outlining the team's purpose and what the team will achieve?
  - *a clear set of priorities* around which team members are focused?

- Is the team sufficiently consistent and aligned, but also diverse in background and experience, and inclusive of different views and others from outside the team?

- Is there adequate time for the team to regularly review its purpose, performance and progress?

- How strong and effective are the norms of team behaviour, and how well does the team deal with setbacks, give feedback, have courageous conversations (do the important things that are often difficult and avoided).

- Do team members hold you and each other to account and in a positive, encouraging way?

- Does your team share experience and expertise?

- How often do you ask the team for feedback, and how effectively do you show team members the behaviours that you want them to show you?

- Are you sensitive enough to team members from cultures other than your own? Do you understand their different context and experience?

- Does your team possess a hierarchy (often informal and tacit)? What are the implications of this?

- Is the team at risk of fragmentation or groupthink?

- Are open, challenging discussions suppressed for fear of alienating 'the boss'?

- Is the team focused on the right things? Is everyone agreed on the priorities and strategy?

- Does the business culture, and do the processes, help or hinder collaboration? What changes would improve the situation?

- How well is team performance monitored? Does the business merely rely on financial indicators or are there other measures?

- Where do tensions typically arise and where are they likely to arise in the future?

- What is the best way to handle and reconcile team tensions when they arise?

- Where is the team succeeding and where does the team need to improve (both individually and as a team)?

- Are objectives and processes aligned, consistent and pulling in the same direction? If not, what needs to change?

- In the last seven days, have team members received recognition or praise for doing good work?

- In the last six months, has someone talked to your team members about their progress?

- In the last year, have you and everyone in your team had opportunities at work to learn and grow?

- Does your team have a learning culture?

- Which of these 20 actions will you do more of or be better at within your team?

1. Sharing lessons and insights, reviewing and feeding back after activities and projects

2. Providing feedback in the moment

3. Formally conducting After Action Reviews (AARs)

4. Encouraging people – from the day they start and at every level of the organization – to ask: 'What have I/we learned today?'

5. Providing less training and more facilitation where people learn by discussing, reflecting and doing

6. Giving employees meta-skills, notably the skills of learning and self-awareness

7. Making learning as personal and relevant for people as possible – for example, by connecting learning with the ability to succeed in a current role and preparing for future ones

8. Recognizing that a desire for learning is not enough: what matters is putting in the effort at the point of need

9. Extending learning interventions over a longer period of time so people can reflect, and apply and review their learning

10. Cutting learning interventions into smaller chunks

11. Asking colleagues to write an action plan and share it (a useful way to focus their thinking and possibly engender commitment)

12. Sharing best practice and celebrating success

13. Developing and engaging stakeholders and line managers – for example, by receiving their input on the vision for the programme or appropriate measures for success

14. Providing access to experts and sources of inspiration and expertise

15. Regularly using a learning journal

16. Offering coaching – either one-to-one or group coaching – as a way of engendering support

17. Developing action learning

18. Sharing experiences from frontline staff and creating job aids for colleagues

19. Strengthening networks and helping people to connect with each other, both inside and outside of their organization, so that they can learn from one another

20. Embedding learning in the business's processes – achieved by starting to think differently about how support and content are provided at the point of need.

## Assessing team performance

As a team leader, your coachee needs to develop a clear understanding of each member of their existing team. The team members can be assessed against four key criteria:

1. **Ability** – do they possess the knowledge, technical competence, experience and sound business judgement to do the job effectively?

2. **Attitude and mindset** – do they have sufficient motivation, energy and focus to do the job, or are they detached from the issues and challenges that you and the business are facing?

3. **Relationships** – are they good team workers, do they work well as part of a team, collaborating and actively supporting corporate and team decisions?

4. **Trust and integrity** – can each member of your team be trusted by you and each other? Will each person do as they say they will?

Performance reviews and other relevant information about each team member should be examined. Any shared 360-degree, multi-rated assessments or surveys will also provide insights. It makes sense for a new team leader to meet members of their team at an early stage, on an individual basis. An informal discussion will help them find out about the person: issues such as their background, family, interests and motivations, as well as views about the work situation. The information an individual recalls will be significant, revealing how they see the work circumstances. Much depends on the team leader's style, but a combination of initial informal meetings and then formal reviews on that person's accountabilities should provide a comprehensive picture.

To assess the team's collective performance and to understand where improvements lie, encourage your coachee to ask whether their team has the following:

- a well-defined purpose, a guiding vision, and strong values

- an understanding of individual responsibilities, relationships, and priorities

- a willingness to subordinate individual goals to group goals

- a cooperative, rather than competitive, climate

- an ability to deal with and appreciate conflict and different points of view

- an understanding of how the team fits in with other teams and with its larger environment

- camaraderie, competence and trust, with resulting high morale

- the ability to keep communication lines open

- a learning culture that values feedback, humility, support and challenge.

In addition, ask the coachee to consider the following:

Are there consistent responses within the team about the way they work?

Are their responses so consistent that they indicate an agreed party line? Or are they so contradictory that they cause you to question consistency and teamwork?

Can the team members work together? Can you work with the team?

## Assessing group dynamics

- If your coachee is a new team leader, get them to observe how the team interacts as soon as possible after their arrival.

- When one person speaks, what is the reaction of others? Their responses can indicate a lot about attitudes, centres of gravity, information, leadership and alliances.

- When you listen, look at what is going on among the other listeners. Who seems to defer to whom, when and why? Do some people distance themselves by looking away – shaking their head or otherwise express disagreement or irritation?

- What are the issues they value?

- Who is most and least vocal – and why?

- What needs to change?

- What needs to be maintained and developed?

## Getting team members' input on key issues

Your coachee should also find out about each person as a team player. They should observe how each individual interacts with them, their boss, the rest of their team, their subordinates and their external contacts. Your coachee should use direct observation and indirect questioning, such as, 'How well does the team work together?' If your coachee decides to conduct systematic structured interviews of their team, they will probably want to ask team members the following questions:

- What are your thoughts about the current strategy?

- What do you see as the biggest challenges in the short term and longer term?

- What are the greatest opportunities – in the short term and longer term?

- What sort of things could we do to be more effective?

- What changes would you make to the way in which the team works?

- If you were me, what things would you be looking at?

The team leader should look at each individual's behaviour: what the person says and what they don't say, as well as what they do and don't do. In particular, they should consider the following:

- What information is volunteered and what information has to be extracted, item by item?

- Do they own their problems or blame others? Are they competent and dynamic?

- Are their relationships with other team members convivial and productive?

- What topics generate an emotional response? Such 'hot buttons issues' can provide clues to motivation and sensitivities that may block or support the changes you may need.

- Are expressions and body language consistent with the words used?

Within a couple of months, the team leader should be able to judge the capabilities and likely futures of team members. The team leader can structure this by allocating existing team members into one of the following categories:

- Who are the **stars** – the high-performing people who should be kept in their current role?

- Who are the **high potentials** – individuals who show potential but need development in their current role?

- Who are the **capable movers** – those people who are capable but would benefit from a move to another position?

- Who is **on probation** – people whose performance gives cause for concern? (The team leader should monitor their performance and agree a personal development plan (PDP) as soon they can.)

- Who are the **low-priority movers** – people to replace in the medium term?

- Who are the **high-priority movers** – people to replace urgently?

## Avoiding pitfalls when restructuring your team

Ask your coachee the following questions if they are planning to reorganize/restructure their team:

- Have you asked other people for their views on your team?

- Are you at risk of being 'captured' by an individual or faction within the team – being excessively persuaded by one person or group?

- Are you clear about which decisions rely on team ownership?

- Do you avoid making decisions requiring team commitment and ownership?

- Do you have appropriate support?

## Managing and leading a team

Your coachee will probably be familiar with the classic stages in the development of teams, as originally proposed by Bruce Tuckman. It can be useful for them to consider their own team in the light of this model. The four-stage model is as follows.

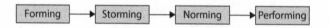

The stages of team development

1. **Forming.** At first, the team is a collection of individuals that are just starting to form into a single unit. The ice is carefully being broken, people are introducing themselves and are generally quiet, getting the measure of others in the team.

2. **Storming.** The team then starts storming: conflict starts to emerge as people display their attitudes and set boundaries. This is an inevitable phase as people get to know others in the team.

3. **Norming.** Next, norms are developed, as people understand each other's strengths, weaknesses and patterns of behaviour. The group functions as a team and tasks are accomplished. Often, teams settle at this level.

4. **Performing.** Finally, the team starts excelling and performing at its very best. This largely results from a steady accumulation of trust, respect and understanding, combined with a common sense of purpose and some successes.

To these four stages can be added a fifth, **reforming**, which is about renewing and reinvigorating the team, perhaps after failures, difficulties or major changes.

To help your coachee reflect on their own team in relation to this model, ask the following questions:

- Do you understand your team's maturity – in particular, what stage of team development are they at (forming, storming, norming, performing or reforming)?

- What are the implications of the team's maturity, experience, membership and their goals?

- What do other people – notably direct reports – think of your team members and their performance?

- How well do you prepare for meetings?

- How could team meetings and other interactions improve?

- Do you walk the talk and do enough to role model the behaviours you expect from your team?

- How well do you listen to your team – not simply what they say but how, when and why they say it?

- Is the team sufficiently focused on external stakeholders and constituents?

- How well do team members communicate?

- How could communications improve?

## CHAPTER 10

# Questions When Coaching across Cultures

As people, organizations and entire economies become more inter-connected than ever before, one of the great benefits of work is to link with people from a culture other than your own. This may be a national culture, but also, an organizational, sectoral or generational culture. This is especially true with coaching; it is an activity that never happens in a vacuum but instead always takes place in the context of individual and cultural beliefs and behaviours. Against this backdrop, of course, a coach brings their own cultural and personal beliefs.

We would suggest that it is impossible to work in another culture successfully without becoming aware and respectful of the history and customs of the place you are in, and the people you are with. When it comes to national culture, for example, the attitudes of the people we come into contact with are profoundly shaped by issues such as education, the history of their country, their politics and their religious beliefs or absence of them.

However, when dealing with culture, it's important to main-tain a balance between paying too much attention, or not enough. Pioneers of cross-cultural studies have provided us with a wealth of frameworks and models. Seminal works by Edward T. Hall, Geert Hofstede and Fons Trompenaars formed the basis of subse-quent studies and research, and we would recommend any coach to read more on this important and fascinating subject (see Notes on Sources and Further Reading).

What coaching universally deals with is enabling people to operate successfully and effectively, while recognizing each individual's different personal background and yet always having to operate within their own culture. Also, it is worth remembering that coaches working within different cultures need to be aware of their own fundamental needs and how they can impact their clients.

Paying attention to information is part of the art of coaching. When someone mentions something, the question is not, '*Why* is this significant?' but, '*How* is this significant?' The art of noticing what is said and asking how it is significant is even more important in cross-cultural coaching than it is when working within one's own culture, where typically we have a much better idea of why things are mentioned and why they are important. Within our own cultures we often generalize about people and situations: we have our own shorthand for shared concepts. In unfamiliar territory, we need to know the landscape and what is shared shorthand, and what that shorthand means to our coachee.

## Questions that build understanding across cultures and contexts

The questions that follow are intended to help coaches who are coaching someone from a culture other than their own. As well as being useful for self-coaching, most are also appropriate and valuable for coaches to ask the person they are working with.

- Are you aware of linguistic issues when communicating across cultures?

- What more can you do to build understanding?

- What actions and words would make people feel at ease and build their trust?

- What actions and words would make people feel uncertain, uncomfortable or concerned?

- What are the most significant events and forces driving the current situation? What is the likely outcome?

- Are you clear about the universal human values, the non-negotiables for you and others?

- What changes and adjustments will you make to succeed in your current environment?

- There is a tendency to think, feel and act in certain innate ways, based on our cultural background. This includes communication, how we perceive oneself and others, problem solving and control. Which of these areas will require you to adjust and alter your approach?

- Are you ready to manage the differences you encounter, as well as acquiring and institutionalizing cultural knowledge, and adapting to the culture of the people you value?

## Insights and questions for people working across national cultures

Cross-cultural diversity presents leaders with dilemmas and conflicts. Leadership is about recognizing, respecting and reconciling these dilemmas. In the view of management writer Fons Trompenaars, as given to this author in an interview, 'Successful leaders have the propensity and competence to help organizations and teams reconcile dilemmas for better global business performance.' Resolving cultural differences typically involves three stages:

1. Awareness of the origins, nature and influence of cultural differences and of culturally defined values and assumptions

2. Respect for cultural differences in style and approach, and an end to stereotyping

3.  Reconciling cultural differences by showing people how to use the strengths of their respective values and approaches.

These differences can be reconciled by:

- looking for opportunities to get more value through each dimension, rather than favouring one or the other, or seeing conflicts between different values

- defining issues in terms of dilemmas, and avoiding compromise

- reaching out to colleagues of different orientations

- a willingness to invest effort in communicating across cultural boundaries

- respecting and practising both generic and local communication practices and business customs.

So, where are the main areas of difference and what are their implications?

## Universalism versus particularism

This cultural conflict concerns the standards by which relationships are measured. For *universalists*, rules and procedures are applied consistently, whereas for *particularists* the relationship and flexibility are more important. Universalists assume that their standards are the right standards and they attempt to change the attitudes of others to match their own. Universalist societies include Switzerland, Canada, USA and Sweden.

Particularist societies are characterized by a belief that the bonds of particular relationships are stronger than abstract rules. Particularist societies include Venezuela, Korea and Russia.

Coaching questions to consider include:

- What do people value in relationships?

- How are relationships developed and measured?

- What actions can you take to build and strengthen relationships?

- What actions would undermine relationships?

- What is the best way to build your network, reputation and personal brand?

- Do people primarily value rules and consistency, or bonds and loyalty?

- Are you open to finding the best way to reconcile the need for consistent rules with the need to be loyal?

## Individualism versus communitarianism

This is about the conflict between an individual's desire and the interests of the group they belong to. In individualist cultures, people are more self-oriented than community-oriented. An individualistic culture emphasizes individual freedom and responsibility. Examples of individualist societies include Israel, Canada and the USA. A communitarian culture emphasizes working for the interests of the group. People are mainly oriented towards common goals and objectives. The communitarian culture is notable in Egypt, Mexico, India and Japan.

Coaching questions to consider include:

- Do people primarily regard themselves as individuals or as part of a group?

- What are the group's values and priorities?

- What are your personal priorities and goals?

- Are you open to finding the best way to reconcile individual and group needs and priorities?

## Neutral versus affective

This focuses on the extent to which people display emotions and on the interaction between reason and emotion in relationships. In neutral cultures, people are taught that it is incorrect to overtly display emotion, whereas in affective cultures people freely express their emotions, even looking for outlets for their feelings. Ethiopia, Japan and China are neutral cultures, whereas Spain, Egypt and Kuwait are affective.

Coaching questions to consider include:

- Do you display too little or too much emotion for the culture in which you operate?

- Would it help to adopt a different approach?

- How effectively do you manage your emotions?

- Are you sufficiently intentional when using your emotions?

- Could you do more to effectively read and manage the emotions of others?

- What is the best way to connect with people and draw them close to you?

- Are you open to finding the best way to reconcile a desire for passion and emotion with a preference for reason and calmness?

## Specific versus diffuse

This dimension involves the way people approach a situation, as well as their degree of involvement in relationships. People from specific-oriented cultures begin by considering each element of a situation, analysing each part separately and then finally putting them back together. The whole is the sum of its parts. Also, people from specific-oriented cultures separate their work from personal relationships. Examples include the Netherlands, Denmark, Sweden and the UK.

In diffuse-oriented cultures people tend to see each element as part of a bigger picture. Also, individuals engage each other across several levels at the same time; elements of life and personality are interwoven. Examples of diffuse societies include China, Nigeria and Kuwait.

Coaching questions to consider include:

- Do you tend to view issues as a whole, or do you break them into separate component parts? Would it help to adopt a different approach?

- Can you see both the wood and the trees – and are you open to finding the best way to reconcile a holistic approach with a recognition of diffuse and different elements?

- Do you understand and pay sufficient attention to the drivers of each issue or person – the forces shaping a particular outcome?

- Do you recognize the overall impact of an issue or person?

## Achievement versus ascription

This focuses on how personal status is assigned. Achieved status relates to an individual's action and what you do (USA, Australia and Canada), whereas ascribed status is more concerned with who you are (Egypt, Argentina, Czech Republic).

Coaching questions to consider include:

- Are you giving sufficient value and recognition to the reasons why someone has the status they do?

- What can be done to enhance someone's position and personal reputation?

- Are you open to finding the best way to reconcile achieved status with bestowed status?

- Are you being fair and supportive?

## Sequential versus synchronic (time orientation)

People in sequential cultures tend to view time as a series of linear, passing events, and they take time and schedule commitment seriously. Synchronic cultures view past, present and future as interrelated – and they usually tend to do several things at once.

Coaching questions to consider include:

- What is the best way to view the passing of time and the arrival of deadlines, as well as the past? In particular, is there consensus on this issue?

- What would help you or your colleague improve your time management?

- Is there a shared perspective on past, present and future issues and events?

## Internal versus external control

This dimension relates to the extent to which people believe they are in control or how much they are affected by their environment.

People who have an internally controlled view tend to believe they can dominate their environment. This contrasts with an externally controlled view of nature, with their actions oriented towards others. They focus on their environment rather than themselves.

Coaching questions to consider include:

- How much control of your environment do you have – is it enough?

- How significant is your environment – can you do more to shape or use the situation you are in?

- Are you focused enough on people or issues? What needs to change?

In summary, when working across national cultures it is important to understand several key points:

- Whereas managers make decisions on issues, high-performing leaders and international managers continually reconcile dilemmas. Transcultural competence is the ability to reconcile seemingly opposing values.

- Creating value means combining issues that are not easily joined and are therefore scarce and profitable.

- Organizational culture is a set of values that drives behaviour.

- Cross-cultural thinking is not linear or a zero-sum game: it requires an ability to handle complexity and reconcile dilemmas.

- Cross-cultural leadership means reconciling and recombining different views, not merely adding or accommodating them.

# CHAPTER 11

# Transformation and Change Questions

Coaching people through periods of transformation, challenge and change, including opportunities as well as unfamiliar issues, difficulties and concerns, is a perennial issue for coaches. It is tempting for each generation to believe that their times may include more change than anyone else. In truth, however, change is a permanent condition, and, given that fact, what matters is our individual ability to accept and embrace change. Given this simple truth, one coaching question stands out: how do you coach people, teams and organizations, so that they do more of the right things and adapt to shifting priorities and new challenges, disruption, opportunities and goals?

The answer lies with empathy, meeting the person where they are and understanding their feelings. Also vitally important is effective leadership, a clear, compelling vision, and the ability to follow through and do the right things, in the right way, at the right time – often described as the ability to execute.

## Supporting people through a period of uncertainty, crisis, disruption, challenge or change

When leading or coaching people through a time of disruption or change (so that would be most of the time) it can help to ask:

- What is the ideal outcome? How can you get there?

- If this issue was resolved, what would the solution look like?

- What would radically change what you do?

- How can you reverse the way you think about this?

- How can you build on the pluses?

- How can you eliminate the minuses?

- What ideas can you borrow, adapt or combine?

- Where are the potential pitfalls and how could these be overcome?

Management writer John Kotter studied 100 companies going through transitions, and by analysing their triumphs and pitfalls he identified several common mistakes as well as an eight-stage process: a sequence of actions that coachees can take to ensure that changes succeed. Each step in Kotter's process for leading change prompts several questions that are useful for anyone leading or coaching people through changing, challenging times.

## 1 Establish a sense of urgency

Organizations frequently allow high levels of complacency to develop during times of transition. Kotter comments: 'Without motivation, people won't help and the effort goes nowhere. Executives underestimate how hard it can be to drive people out of their comfort zones.' A 'burning platform' (or a 'melting iceberg', less visible but equally perilous) is a valuable way to remove complacency and inertia. Key coaching questions at this stage include:

- What are the priorities?

- What is the reason for the change?

- What will happen if things stay the same?

- What is the vision – the ideal outcome?

- What is the strategy – the route to moving from where we are now to where we want to be?

- How will the required/desired changes be perceived? What is the likely response?

- What is the best way to communicate the need for change and establish a sense of urgency? How will this be done, and who will do it?

## 2 Form a guiding coalition

A strong, unified group should drive the change process and establish support throughout the entire organization or business. Key coaching questions at this stage include:

- Who is best placed to drive forward the change?

- How will this happen?

- What are the potential pitfalls?

- Is there an established process or team that could be used to guide people through the change?

- Who will lead?

## 3 Create a vision

A clear sense of direction and an idea of the end result will allow efforts to be focused, organized and efficient. Key coaching questions include:

- What is the vision – the ideal outcome?

- What will success look like?

- What will a successful outcome mean for the organization, each team and each individual?

- How will you get people to buy into the vision and use it to guide their actions?

- What stories or metaphors can you use to provide guiding examples?

## 4 Communicate the vision

The strategy and vision for change must be communicated to everyone involved. As well as holding discussions and using other forms of communication, members of the guiding coalition should act as role models for the type of behaviours and decisions that are needed. Key coaching questions include:

- How will you connect with people's hearts and minds? How will you move them to action?

- What is the message, and what is the media you will use to reach people?

- How will you ensure consistent communication?

- What will people want to know?

- Great communication is two-way – it requires listening as well as telling. So, how will you listen, and how will you act on what you hear?

- How will you share updates and sustain progress?

### 5 Empower others to act on the vision

If old procedures and obstacles remain in place during change it will likely be discouraging for employees involved in the effort. So, encourage and support people to make the right changes, ideally, without always referring upwards. Key questions include:

- Are you encouraging, reassuring and rewarding people when they make progress, or even when they try?

- Are people empowered? Are they clear about what they need to achieve – their accountabilities?

- What limits are there to people's authority? When is escalation likely to be needed?

- What needs to change?

### 6 Plan for and create short-term victories

Find ways to start the process and work hard to generate momentum, even in small ways. Motivate employees by continuously emphasizing milestones and successes. Accentuate the positive aspects of the transition. Key coaching questions include:

- What should change first – is there a plan with roles assigned?

- Where is the low-hanging fruit – the totemic changes that will provide an exemplar and signal things to come?

- How do you build and sustain momentum? What do others think would be the best way to do this?

- What are the milestones on the way to making the changes you need?

## 7 Consolidate improvements and maintain momentum

Rather than growing complacent as the process develops, use the credibility gained to reinvigorate and expand the changes to all areas of the company. Key coaching questions include:

- How can you consolidate the gains you have achieved? How will you ensure things don't go back to how they were?

- What next – having been successful in one area, where can you logically and most effectively go next (so as to sustain momentum and progress)?

## 8 Institutionalize the new approaches

Anchor the changes firmly in the culture of the organization. Changes are most effective when they become entrenched. Key coaching questions include:

- How will you share the shifts and changes with key stakeholders, including customers?

- How will you use the changes to provide added value?

- Do you have the right measures in place?

- Does the culture need shaping or altering in any way?

## Ensuring progress and overcoming problems during times of transformation and change

The unfamiliarity that comes with change can provide excitement or, more usually, it can prompt concern. This concern leads, in turn, to self-doubt, resistance, possible fear, and what is best described as immunity to change. The questions below are intended to coach someone so they can understand and get past their immunity to change.

- Achieving transformational change requires sustained commitment as well as practical support. Is this in place? Is it strong, authentic and committed?

- What are the barriers to change? How will these be overcome and addressed?

- The following list can help to identify barriers to changing. Which of the following issues are of greatest significance for your organization? Barriers can often occur if people:
  ◦ tend to follow rather than initiate
  ◦ like the status quo
  ◦ tend to react and not think ahead
  ◦ lack confidence
  ◦ follow the path of least resistance
  ◦ avoid risk
  ◦ do not encourage or value new ideas
  ◦ believe urgency has priority over importance
  ◦ take a top-down approach to communication
  ◦ have little time to think
  ◦ provide limited support for change
  ◦ receive few rewards for innovation.

- If you were to prioritize each barrier or source of resistance, which issues:
  a) are you able to change now?
  b) are beyond your scope to change – but which you can influence?
  c) are you unable to change or influence at this stage?

Work on issues that lead to As and Bs, and discuss with colleagues how to resolve organizational barriers that cause Cs.

- Is there more you can do to find new ideas and creative ways to enhance performance?

- Would it be useful to:
  - establish a project team to identify new ideas, or include this aspect as a regular agenda item at team meetings?
  - organize a team 'away day' to focus on new ideas and issues (e.g. winning new customers, improving processes or reducing costs)?
  - find out about scenario planning, a technique that can help to create new ideas and perspectives?
  - establish a coaching culture?
  - clearly define strategic goals?
  - get the top team aligned with the need for a coaching culture to support these goals?
  - communicate these goals and explain how they will be achieved?

- Do you need to provide people with the skills and development to succeed in the new, changing and altering environment?

- How often will you review progress and make changes?

## Dos and don'ts when leading people through change

When it comes to helping people through times of change, there is a wide range of pitfalls and dysfunctional behaviours awaiting coaches and leaders. Which of these dos and don'ts are you most susceptible to as a coach? Which ones are the most significant for your coachee?

**Do:**

- Identify areas that require change and identify appropriate change initiatives.

- Take into account the concerns of major stakeholders.

- Develop a change project plan covering project team, activities, timescale, measurements, communications and feedback.

- Encourage people to change, and show them how to do things differently.

- Communicate the benefits, and develop a shared sense of purpose.

- Overcome obstacles and remove any constraints (bureaucracy or procedures) that block action.

- Accept the need for training and development, and plan relevant activities.

- Ensure that all parts of the business support the changes (including systems such as personnel, finance and IT).


**Do not:**

- Avoid problems or ignore frustrations.

- Take a back seat, but display commitment and determination.

- Lose people's confidence.

- Ignore the need to set an example by what you do as well as what you say.

- Fail to actively listen to people or adjust your thinking.

## Adaptive or technical?

One of the biggest failures of managers is to treat adaptive challenges like technical problems, even though each has their own solutions.

- Which of your coachee's challenges are adaptive, and which ones are technical? Focus your coachee (or focus yourself) on a challenge, problem, opportunity or issue you face, and decide if it is adaptive or technical.

- Is it a technical issue? What is the way to plan and implement your solution? Who needs to be involved, what needs to be done and what is the desired outcome?

- If it is an adaptive issue, what are the most significant and challenging elements, and what is the best way to approach them?

| Technical problems... | ...and adaptive challenges |
|---|---|
| Easy to identify | Difficult to identify (easy to deny) |
| Often lend themselves to quick and easy solutions | Require changes in values, beliefs, roles, relationships, and approaches to work |
| Can often be solved by an authority or expert | People with the problem do the work of solving it |

| Technical problems... | ...and adaptive challenges |
|---|---|
| Require change in just one or a few places; often contained within organizational boundaries | Require change in numerous places; usually cross organizational boundaries |
| People are generally receptive to technical solutions | People often resist even acknowledging adaptive challenges |
| Solutions can often be implemented quickly – even by edict | 'Solutions' require experiments and new discoveries; they can take a long time to implement and cannot be implemented by edict |

## Coaching questions for the checked-out and disengaged

If colleagues are not sufficiently engaged, we clearly need to understand why and do something about it and, perhaps counter-intuitively, a sensible approach is to first look at oneself. Are you, as leader, the reason for a lack of engagement, a sense of frustration or simple detachment? It may be useful to acknowledge that brilliant bosses work hard at several things consistently and effectively – and in particular they make work meaningful and enjoyable for employees. In fact, leaders are most successful when they adhere to a few simple practices. If you are managing someone who is disengaged, asking that person some coaching questions may help them.

### Questions for the coach or manager of someone who is disengaged

Useful questions to ask oneself include:

Why is this person behaving this way – what changed?

Do I have the full picture – are there things happening elsewhere in this person's life that might be having an effect? If so, what are they, and what's the best approach?

What does this person want and need?

What are the potential consequences of this person's behaviour, and are they aware of these?

What is the room for manoeuvre here – where can we be more flexible and accommodating?

## Manage individuals, not just teams

When you're under pressure it is easy to forget that employees have varying interests, abilities, goals and styles of learning. Take time to check in on people and understand what makes each person tick so that you can customize your interactions with them.

- How are things going?

- How do you feel?

- How are things generally – at home, in other areas of your life?

- Is everything OK – what's on your mind?

- Is anything bothering you?

- How do you feel about [*a recent activity or event, national or international; something within the organization or ecosystem; or something more personal*]?

## Purpose matters: go big on meaning

- Inspire people with a vision, set challenging goals and articulate a clear purpose. Don't rely on incentives or socializing.

- How do you feel about [*describe the vision, strategy, project or big-picture goal*]?

- What excites you?

- How motivated do you feel right now? (OR How motivated do you feel about [*mention an issue*]?)

- What is the significance, impact or benefit of your work? What does it bring you?

- What would an ideal day looks like?

## Provide constructive feedback

Use regular (at least weekly) one-on-one conversations for coaching. Make the feedback clear, honest and constructive; it's a great way to show someone that they are valued.

- You seem [*describe the behaviour you have see*] – why is that?

- How are things going this week?

- What have you learned?

- What have you achieved?

- Who benefited from your work?

- What went well, and what didn't?

## Listen – don't just talk

- Tell me, what's on your mind? I'm keen to understand.

- What do you need?

- What would help?

- Is there anything I can do?

## Be consistent

- Be open to new ideas in your management style, vision, expectations and feedback. If change becomes necessary, acknowledge it quickly.

- What aspects of work would you like to change?

- Give me feedback – how am I doing?

- It may help to check in on the same issues, regularly. What issues should we cover each week?

## Finally, be self-aware

Understand your own strengths and areas for improvement, your impact and the shadow you cast as a leader and your values, and know what you want to accomplish.

## Getting people to realize their potential and step up

It helps to start by genuinely acknowledging someone's potential, their past successes, the valuable attributes they bring that were the reason they became part of the organization in the first place and their strengths. This has several benefits: it makes you feel more positive, at a time when you may be overcome with frustration or disappointment; and it goes some way to establishing rapport. It shows you are trying to be open, honest and constructive from the start. This initial level of honest, genuine support and rapport then gives you permission to challenge their behaviour – for example, by asking:

- You aren't operating at your full potential – for example... Why is this? What's holding you back?

- You seem detached – why?

- I'm keen for you to stretch and develop your skills – what do you suggest?

- What do you think you are capable of achieving?

- What motivates you?

- Where do you see yourself in one, three and ten years' time?

- How are things going? Is everything OK?

- What can I do to help you?

- What do you need to get better at?

- What do you enjoy, and what do you dislike, about your current role?

- How do you feel about the team role/project/current challenge – what would improve things?

- How would you like to be remembered – what would you like your legacy to be?

- What's been your greatest success?

## Increasing team engagement and performance

The questions below will help you focus on the challenge of increasing engagement. Consider to what extent they apply to members of your team.

- Is the team focused on the right things? Is everyone agreed on the priorities and strategy?

- Does the business culture and the processes help or hinder collaboration? What changes would improve the situation?

- How well is performance monitored? Does the business merely rely on financial indicators or are there other measures?

- Where do tensions typically arise, and where are they likely to arise in the future?

- What is the best way to handle and reconcile tensions when they arise?

- Where is the team succeeding, and where do we need to improve (individually, and as a team)?

In every case there should be a constructive and genuine approach, empathy, and positive intent. This is often tough to achieve with the checked-out and disengaged. And kindness and empathy usually, but not always, work better than anything else.

Remember, the ability to guide people through changing, unfamiliar and even fearful times is one of the defining skills of a leader. In fact, it is inescapable, and it is best done positively, rigorously, and with a spirit of openness, optimism, curiosity and fun.

**CHAPTER 12**

# Communication, Influencing and Engagement Questions

Successfully coaching someone so that they are more influential and effective as a leader relies, in large part, on the coach's ability to help someone embrace the need for skilful, appropriate communications. So, what makes an engaging, influential communication? The first point should be obvious: have something clear, appealing and compelling to offer. Beyond this fundamental point, great communicators have several useful tools and techniques that work as well today, in the digital age, as they ever have. In fact, it can be said that technology goes a long way to support, develop and amplify emotional connections.

## Achieving better communication

Great coaches are skilful, powerful communicators themselves, and they help their coachee find their own style. A good starting point is to help the coachee recognize that communications divide broadly into two areas: written and spoken. So, how can we, as leaders and coaches, be better at both? Several thoughts may help.

### Give of oneself, be personal, and show your passion

This helps you to build rapport and trust and give your audience confidence in your words. Simply put, it means help your listeners get to know you, for example by giving personal insights into your own life.

There are several notable examples: in his books, many of his interviews and even in his formal speeches, Barack Obama often refers to his wife and children; Martin Luther King's 'I have a dream' speech mentions his children in one of the most famous lines of the twentieth century: 'I have a dream that my four little children will one day live in a nation where they will not be judged by the colour of their skin, but by the content of their character.'

### 'Own' the communication – believe your words

This matters for several reasons – first, because people value genuineness and 'authenticity', and, second, people are so used to hearing speeches and seeing messages that they have got much better at sensing when people are not genuine (unlike, for example, a hundred years ago).

### Show empathy, understand your audience and appeal to their values

Who are your constituents? What do they think or want? How are they likely to respond? What do you want from them and how can you get this? For example, Winston Churchill understood during the Second World War that the British people wanted a confident, defiant, resolute leader, and a sense of clarity and purpose.

### Be honest and fair; remember, people everywhere respond well to universal values

These include honesty, reasonableness and courage: typically, we want them for ourselves and we value them in others. So, when you speak, show that you are a decent member of the human race.

### Master the essentials

In particular:

- Prepare – don't assume it is easy and don't take your audience for granted. Understand them.

- Be yourself and be appropriate. If you are authentically yourself, so will your audience be; if you are fretful, fearful or distracted that is how they will be.

- Give your communication a clear theme or message.

- Provide illustrations and examples.

- When speaking, pause – give your audience time to think.

- Ask questions – they are a great way to command attention and engagement.

- Remember that great communications inspire by being personal, bold, ambitious and attractive. Not mediocre, impersonal or confusing.

Finally, if appropriate, ask your audience to do something or think about something – how can we...? Why don't we...? What will you do to...?

## Questions for communicators

The following questions will help if you are coaching someone to improve their effectiveness as a communicator.

- What is your message? What do you want to say?

- Why do you want to convey your message? Why is it important, and how passionate are you about this?

- What response and outcome are you looking for? What is the vision?

- What is your intended purpose – is it worth being explicit about this?

- Who is your primary audience? Who else do you need to appeal to?

- What are your audience's priorities? What is their situation, their state of mind?

- What will attract people to: a) engage with your message in the first place? b) respond to your message?

- What is the most appropriate way to convey your message – what 'medium' is best?

- What are the competing voices that your message will need to overcome?

- What issues do you need to address?

- What examples can you use?

- What is expected of you?

- When is the best time to communicate?

- Positive values of inspiration and optimism are better motivators for people than negative emotions of fear – what tone do you want to convey?

- What do you do well when you communicate, and where are your personal failings or pitfalls?

- Are you listening – or ready to listen – to the response to your communication? How will this work in practice?

- If your message is contentious, how will you persuade people – how will you appeal to them and win them over?

- What are the potential pitfalls that you may need to overcome?

- How will you engage your audience emotionally (if appropriate)?

- How will you sustain or follow up the communication?

## Helping someone get their message across: building positive, assertive, influential relationships

A perennial challenge when coaching in business is helping leaders to develop assertive and influential relationships – the kind that are full of positive intent, genuine support and constructive challenge, and that deliver results alongside productive relationships.

It is useful to consider the behaviour of yourself and others, in terms of warmth or coldness, dominance or submissiveness. These characteristics underpin four leadership behaviours: aggressive, assertive, avoiding or appeasing.

- **Warm** means being supportive, open, positive, empathic, constructive and engaging – not simply friendly.

- **Dominant** is about being challenging, in control, confident, strong, authoritative and direct.

- **Assertive** means influencing people and combining appropriate levels of challenge and support.

- **Submissive** means being appeasing, keen to please and fit in, as well as uncomfortable or unwilling to confront or challenge.

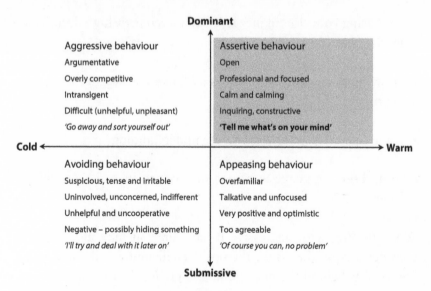

**Dominant**

Aggressive behaviour
Argumentative
Overly competitive
Intransigent
Difficult (unhelpful, unpleasant)
*'Go away and sort yourself out'*

Assertive behaviour
Open
Professional and focused
Calm and calming
Inquiring, constructive
**'Tell me what's on your mind'**

**Cold** ← → **Warm**

Avoiding behaviour
Suspicious, tense and irritable
Uninvolved, unconcerned, indifferent
Unhelpful and uncooperative
Negative – possibly hiding something
*'I'll try and deal with it later on'*

Appeasing behaviour
Overfamiliar
Talkative and unfocused
Very positive and optimistic
Too agreeable
*'Of course you can, no problem'*

**Submissive**

Leadership behaviours

The figure above, based on the Thomas–Kilmann Conflict Mode Instrument, highlights different types of behaviour displayed both by the leader and the person they are working with. It is the role of the leader to recognize the individual's behaviour and modify their own approach so as to reach agreement.

It is important to remember that every leader has their own personality, the result both of nature and nurture, and this remains largely unchanged. However, behaviour is different: it is flexible and capable of being developed and enhanced.

## Aggressive: cold and dominant behaviour

Aggressive individuals are often argumentative, unreasonable and hostile. Their aggression tends to result from too much dominance and too little warmth or support. Consequently, they always seem to know best and typically demonstrate defiance, competitiveness, hostility and sarcasm.

When dealing with aggressive behaviour, the best approach involves:

- increasing your dominance levels to match their high dominance levels

- ensuring that your behaviour is assertive and warm rather than aggressive

- using open questions to generate understanding

- using body language and tone of voice to increase dominance levels.

When dealing with aggressive behaviour, you may also want to consider 'taking the lid off the pot' – challenging and confronting the reasons behind the behaviour, and giving clear examples.

### Avoiding: cold and submissive behaviour

People who display an avoiding style are cold and submissive. They tend to be suspicious, uninvolved, indifferent, tense, hard to read, withdrawn and pessimistic. They may also show signs of being calculating.

When dealing with cold and submissive behaviour, the first priority is to get people engaged. Useful techniques include:

- displaying lower dominance and higher warmth

- using open questions aimed at making them feel secure

- softening body language and intonation while continuing to smile.

### Appeasing: warm and submissive behaviour

Appeasing behaviour is also ineffective. Individuals displaying this behaviour tend to be overly friendly and inclined to ramble. They are often too agreeable; making big promises, being optimistic and dodging confrontation.

When dealing with appeasing behaviour, the first priority is to professionalize the discussion. Invariably greater focus needs to be given to the issue or result, and less to the relationship. There are several techniques to help you achieve this and deal effectively with warm and submissive behaviour:

- Stay focused to keep them on track

- Use open questions that appeal to their social needs but temper these with closed questions when they waffle. Closed questions are useful for controlling social interaction

- Ask summary questions to maintain clarity and focus

- Use their name if you're interrupting.

## Assertive: warm and dominant behaviour

You should aim to have both your behaviour and that of the person you are influencing in the assertive quadrant. When dealing with warm and dominant behaviour:

- Make sure that your dominance and warmth are appropriate, matching the other person

- Use open and closed questions to ensure progress and focus

- Use clear, productive communications that keep the focus on both the relationship and result.

Consider how easy it is to warm up behaviour:

- Why and when is it not easy?

- Why do we, as individuals, not behave in an assertive manner?

- What is it that hinders supportive and challenging behaviour?

- Finally, what are the most important questions for you to ask?

## Matching coaching questions to behaviours

If you are coaching someone who is aggressive, avoiding, appeasing or successfully assertive – or if you are coaching a leader who is themself having to deal with these behaviours – then the following questions will be useful.

### Dealing with aggressive (cold and dominant) behaviour

The priority here is to match the individual's level of dominance and challenge by asking questions, and also, counter-intuitively when faced with someone who is aggressive, to warm up the relationship and show them you have a shared interest.

- What's wrong? What's the matter – can I help?

- There's something on your mind – what do you need?

- You seem a little off – what's wrong?

- You don't seem yourself – is everything OK?

- You seem quite aggressive – what's bothering you?

- Did you know you come across as [a little] aggressive?

- That sounds tough, harsh – what makes you say that?

- Do you think that's the best tone or approach to take to get this thing done?

- I can see you feel strongly about this – tell me what's on your mind?

## Dealing with avoiding (cold, submissive and uninterested) behaviour

These questions are high when it comes to warmth – you need the other person to know that you are on their side and you need to build the relationship. They are also encouraging and slightly challenging: the person needs to know that they are capable of more, and could push themselves further than they are.

- You seem preoccupied, detached, uninterested – why? What's wrong?

- I sense we're not getting your A-game here – you seem detached, like something is on your mind. What's wrong?

- I think you can do better – what's your view? What's holding you back?

- There's something on your mind – what would help?

- I don't think you're completely on board – is there a problem?

- You're better than this, I've seen it! What's holding you back?

## Dealing with appeasing behaviour and people who are talkative, rambling and overly keen to please

These questions would typically be cooler and, unusually, may even be closed. Appeasers need lots of challenge and not too much warmth, although assertiveness always demands some warmth and positivity. The issue here is that the individual is too focused on the relationship and little else.

- When will you complete that?

- How will you complete it?

- When do you think you will you start to show progress with this issue?

- What help or resources do you need?

- What's the plan, timescale and milestones?

- What will 'good' look like?

- What are the likely issues and how are you going to approach/resolve them?

## Developing skills of assertion and influence

Several elements are important here. First, provide a role model for the behaviour you want to see; in other words, be warm and establish connection and rapport, but also remember the need to focus, challenge and push to receive the best possible result in the right way and at the right time. A wide range of questions can help, and they all have an element of support and warmth, combined with challenge and focus. For example:

- What's the goal?

- What would be ideal?

- What's stopping you?

- How can you do that faster/more cheaply/better/more easily... ?

- What's the vision – the outcome you want to achieve?

- What are the potential obstacles?

- Whose help or support do you need?

- What resources would be useful or needed?

- What's on your mind?

- What's the problem?

- How can we solve it?

- What are the issues here?

- What would help?

- What are the benefits of success?

- What are the potential consequences of failure?

- What could go wrong?

- What do you need to do to ensure success?

- What are the components or drivers of a successful outcome?

- Is this a choice between 'least bad' options?

- Are there examples that would help guide or inform you?

## Engaging and mobilizing people

Coaching someone so that they are a more engaging leader – someone better able to mobilize people and unlock their loyalty and commitment – is a vital, valuable skill, especially when working with senior executives. This is because engaging and mobilizing people is a vital, defining role for a leader – everyone needs to be able to do it at some point in their leadership career, and the people they need to mobilize could include team members, colleagues, stakeholders, senior managers or members of the wider community. When coaching someone to be more effective at mobilizing people, several principles are useful:

### 1 Make sure you have a compelling vision – a positive outcome in mind that will guide actions and inspire commitment

This is not just relevant for big-picture thinking, grand ideas and strategies; it works particularly well for projects and smaller tasks.

- What do you want to achieve and why? What is it that you want people to do?

- What will good look like?

- Is there a 'burning platform' or a 'melting iceberg' – an essential, compelling, unarguable reason to act?

- Does the vision provide clear and specific guidance about what needs to be achieved – the outcome – and any other relevant issues such as deadlines, milestones, sources of support?

- Do people clearly understand and accept *why* the goal matters?

- Is the desired outcome an end goal (e.g. achieve a sales target) or is it a performance goal (e.g. improve)?

- Is there adequate commitment, or is this somewhere you need to provide help and focus?

- Have you agreed the timescale and milestones?

- Is there a risk of being too prescriptive? This can be a problem as too much prescription can be disempowering or confusing.

- What will success look like for the organization and the individual?

## 2 Understand and empathize with the people you need to mobilize

- Who do you need to get on board – and why?

- What are the different groups or constituencies that you need to engage? What do you have in common, and how do they differ?

- Whose buy-in or action is essential, and who else needs to know about or support your goal?

- What are the benefits for this group (or for each individual)? What's in it for them?

## 3 Appeal to each group, or each individual – and remember, sometimes you need to 'sell the sizzle'

- What is the context and what are their situations? Specifically, what are the priorities, aspirations, preferences, needs and concerns of the people you need to get on board?

- What is the most important thing happening for these people – and how will your message affect this and be received by them?

- What do they want to hear? What do they expect to hear?

- How well are you listening to them and taking their situation on board? What evidence do you have for this?

- What are the key messages you need to get across?

- What would stun, excite or 'wow' your audience? Or, if it's more appropriate, what would they truly welcome and value? How could you make them cheer, like and share your ideas?

**4 Be aware that the message is only part of the battle – what also matters is the media (how you communicate) and the timing**

- What is the best way to reach this group? For example, is it: in person – for example, at a town hall meeting – via social media, one-to-one, through connections and viral word of mouth, online, using TV, or something else?

- How will you engage the group or individual in dialogue? What are the questions to ask, the areas on which to focus, and the best tools to do this?

- When is the best moment to connect with each individual or group? What makes this the best time?

- When might it be wrong, counterproductive or inappropriate to give your message?

**5 Be ready to engage and move people with the power of emotion**

- How will you engage people emotionally? How can you connect with their feelings and perceptions – what they know, do and believe?

- How can you make the need to act 'real' – a priority? In particular, can you make the need to act tangible or experiential?

- What can you do or show people that will command their attention and desire to act?

- What is often most effective at mobilizing people is not just telling but *showing*. How can you do this most effectively?

**6 Use your words thoughtfully; in particular, be open and – if relevant – personal.**

- Are there examples or stories you can share which illustrate your point?

- Can you provide personal stories that will engage and draw in your audience?

- Is humour appropriate?

- Which aspects of your personality and approach do you want to emphasize?

- What words will you use?

- What tone do you want to strike?

- Have you practised or shared your words with anyone in advance, inviting comment or feedback?

- How well-structured is your communication? Do you, for example, provide context, the main body of your message, stories and examples, and finish with a call to action?

- What is your call to action – is it clear what you want people to do?

## 7 Be ready to overcome objections

- What obstacles, risks and concerns will people have?

- What are people's likely concerns?

- How will concerns be expressed? In particular, is there an opportunity for people to express their views or concerns?

- Are concerns and objections valid?

- Is it useful to acknowledge other views and take into account other perspectives?

- How will you address and counter likely objections?

- It can be helpful to acknowledge people's likely feelings and concerns, ask for something (time, their support, faith in your approach or team), and answer their deepest held concerns or appeal to their needs and priorities. Would it help to adopt this approach?

- Whose support do you need to address or overcome objections?

## 8 Use incentives and be realistic

- What would motivate this group or person to act?

- What would win hearts and minds? Is there a 'quid pro quo' arrangement that would galvanize someone to act?

- How will you develop and sustain momentum? Can you build on confidence, experience, expertise or success?

## 9 Be decent and human

Remember, it is not just what we do that matters, but how we do it.

- What competing priorities does this group have?

- What are the potential obstacles or difficulties?

- How can these challenges be overcome?

- Are there success measures or milestones that you can track and highlight?

- How will you recognize progress and celebrate success?

## Sustaining team engagement and performance

The following questions will help if you are coaching someone with the challenge of increasing engagement and focus – a tough issue and a vital one for leaders at all levels. Consider to what extent they apply to members of your coachee's team. Where could they improve and what action will they take?

Ask your coachee:

- Is the team focused on the right things? Is everyone agreed on the priorities and strategy?

- Does the business culture and processes help or hinder collaboration? What changes would improve the situation?

- How well is performance monitored? Does the business merely rely on financial indicators or are other measures?

- Where do tensions typically arise and where are they likely to arise in the future?

- What is the best way to handle and reconcile tensions when they arise?

- Where is the team succeeding and where do we need to improve (individually, and as a team)?

- Are objectives and processes aligned, consistent and pulling in the same direction? If not, what needs to change?

- In the last seven days, have team members received recognition or praise for doing good work?

- In the last six months, has someone talked to your team members about their progress?

- In the last year, have you and everyone in your team had opportunities at work to learn and grow?

- Finally, ask the coachee which aspect of communication is their greatest strength, and what do they need to improve? Remember to help them maximize strengths and recognize the things they can do better.

# PART 3

# Coaching Questions for Defining Moments of Leadership

Coaching is often most needed, requested and, as a result, effective at specific moments during a career, and these can be large (e.g. taking on a new role) or relatively small (e.g. completing a specific task or project). The following chapters focus on the most significant situations where the support and challenge of a great coach can provide the greatest benefit. These situations frequently arise in organizations worldwide, as well as being the areas where individuals and organizations often look to coaches for support.

# CHAPTER 13

# Arrival Questions

Helping someone succeed in a new role is a perennial coaching challenge – and it can start even before the new role begins. When someone is starting a new job, it can help to focus their first month on finding out as much as they can about the organization, the people, and the role. Soon after your coachee has begun their new role, review plans and performance data. Encourage them to look through recent reviews for all of their direct reports, meet with each of them one-on-one and ask about their view of the team and where it needs to go.

## Getting to know and understand people and situations

While your coachee is taking in all of this information, be sure they develop hypotheses about what they need to get done and the best way to go about it. Help them to use the time and unique situation to begin asking questions – a habit that should continue. It can help to start by questioning the coachee's own approach as they prepare for your new role. For example:

- What information do you need before starting your new role? How can you acquire this information quickly?

- What are likely to be the most significant working relationships? Can you start building these before you take up your new role?

- How much time do you plan to set aside for yourself and your family?

- If you are moving location, what will you do to get to know your new environment?

- What expectations do you have – what do you want to achieve – and what are your boss's expectations? Are these reasonable?

- Can you manage expectations so that you achieve what is possible, while allowing yourself to excel and to exceed expectations?

- Are you aware of your leadership and decision-making style?

- Do you know how your behaviour affects others, and do you have the right style, mindset and attitude?

- Have you set time aside to understand the issues and plan your approach to the new role?

- Are you leaving your current role in a professional and supportive way, giving your successor the same support that you will need in your new role?

- Do you have a balanced and clear perspective about the business – its strengths and weaknesses, products, markets, customers, people and opportunities?

- Are you ready to engage people in your new role?

- Are you prepared to build coalitions with others? This is essential if you are to identify and achieve early wins.

- What long-term changes might be needed?

- Do you have a broad timescale for what you would like to achieve, and the actions needed to accomplish this?

- Are you ready to develop a vision for the business – a view of the future to guide people's actions, to challenge and inspire individuals and to appeal to customers and other stakeholders?

- Have you assessed your own weaknesses?

- Is there a mentor or coach you could work with to support you during the transition and to help you achieve your aims?

## Be clear and intentional about how you want to be

Help your coachee decide what the priorities are and then help them to think through what they need to develop, change, do differently, the limiting beliefs they need to overcome, and what their leadership style will mean in practice.

- What sort of leader do you aspire to be?

- What personal qualities would you like to characterize your leadership?

- What will you do more or better – and how?

- What do you want people to say about you?

Understand what they need to do to succeed in their current role, and to prepare for the next one.

This trick was expertly described in the book *The Leadership Pipeline* by Ram Charan, Stephen Drotter and James Noel. Explain to your coachee that they need to be clear about the baseline for the job, the essentials, as well as what outcomes will make them exceptional in the role. Then, help them to think through the skills and behaviours they need to develop and demonstrate now, if they are to progress to the next role. Ask them:

- What will success in the role look like for you? For your boss?

- What are your objectives?

- Start with the end in mind: what do you want your legacy to be?

## Start by building trust

Most leaders emphasize their competence, strength and credentials, but none of that matters if people don't trust you. Help your coachee win people over with warmth. Here's how – encourage them to:

- Pay attention to your body language and use the right tone. Aim for a tone that suggests that you're levelling with people and being completely honest.

- Validate feelings. If you show your employees that you hold roughly the same worldview they do, you demonstrate not only empathy but, in their eyes, common sense. If you want colleagues to listen and agree with you, first agree with them.

- Be warm, smile – and mean it. Smiling is contagious. When people see you beaming, they'll likely smile too. But a polite grin fools no one. To project warmth, you have to genuinely feel it.

## Prepare a professional personal portrait

It will help your coachee to plan in advance how they will present themself: their career history, experience, successes, interests, aspirations – the kind of person they are. Encourage them to be open, engaging and real, and, crucially, prepared.

## Set routines

Point out to your coachee that routines are a great way to ease oneself into a role; they not only help you but also your family and colleagues as well. They can also help an individual stay balanced at a time when they may be pulled in different directions.

## Set short- and long-term goals

It's important to know what 'good' will look like: the results that need to be achieved and also the things they want to accomplish. Life is about choices, especially at the senior level. So, what is your coachee choosing to prioritise? In particular, focus on the goals they want to achieve in the first:

- 30 days

- three months

- year.

...and by the time you move on to the next role. These goals should be specific, measurable, attainable, relevant (for both your career and, of course, for the organization) and timely (SMART – see Introduction, page 15).

## Be confident and clear about strengths

As you coach, keep in mind that confidence – both yours and your coachee's – isn't something you either have or you don't. It's a dynamic emotion that needs exercise to grow stronger and can diminish if neglected. Here are two ways to build and maintain confidence. First, take inventory of your past. It's easy to doubt yourself and your abilities. But if you look at your track record, chances are that your successes outweigh your failures. And, more importantly, you likely survived your missteps and gleaned lessons along the way. Second, focus on your strengths. Most leaders are very strong in a few competencies, average in the majority, and weak in a few. Concentrate on leveraging what you're best at. Then, manage your average and weak areas so they don't detract from your effectiveness.

### Find and pick the low-hanging fruit

Nothing succeeds (or generates momentum) like success. So, help your coachee find out what will make the most impact in the easiest/cheapest/fastest way, and then set about delivering that. One tip: an after action review can help set the tone for the future – showing that learning is vital and continuous, as well as enabling them to build on that initial success (see Chapter 14).

### Remember the three people to talk to when starting a new job

Often there is so much new information that it's difficult to know where to focus. In this situation it can help to speak early with:

- **Frontline employees.** People who develop and deliver products or deliver can familiarize you with the organization's basic processes and relationships with key customers.

- **Networkers and integrators.** Colleagues who coordinate interaction across functions (e.g. HR, finance or plant managers) can tell you how different areas connect with each other – or how they don't. They can shed light on the true political hierarchies.

- **Company historians.** Look for colleagues who have been with the firm for a long time. They'll be able to teach you about the company's mythology and the roots of its culture.

## Develop your influence by listening

People don't like being pushed, or even nudged, to do something. So when you need others to take action – change behaviour, adopt a new strategy – inspire them to commit rather than forcing them to get on board. The best way to do this is to listen, without your own needs and biases getting in the way. Try to understand where your colleagues are coming from. Resist the urge to defend yourself, explain yourself or offer quick fixes. You can help more effectively later, when the time is right, if you don't pre-judge what they need (which might be very different from what you think). Instead, remember that you are listening to learn. Ask questions like: What does that mean for you? How do you feel about it? What's your perspective on it? This is listening of the highest order.

## Build a strong relationship with your new boss

Your boss has more impact than any other person on your success or failure at work. When starting a new job, it pays to invest in this relationship. Here's how to start the right way. First, don't stay away. Even if the boss gives you a lot of freedom, resist the urge to take it. Get on your manager's calendar regularly to communicate any issues you're facing and gather their input. Also, assume they want to focus on the most important things you're trying to do, and how they can help. Focus on no more than three things in each meeting. Finally, clarify expectations early and often. Start during the interview process then check in regularly to make sure they haven't shifted.

## Delegate successfully – in the right way from the start

Many new managers start by delegating poorly, creating problems for the future. It is vital to get this right from the start. Here are suggestions for improving the delegation process and avoiding the label of micromanagement:

### Delegate the problem, don't solve it

The first sign of micromanaging is when delegating a project you also delegate the specifics of the solution. While that makes sense in some fields, in creative or information work, being told up front the steps to follow makes one feel like a vendor and not a partner in the work. This type of delegation doesn't have the feeling that it enhances skills or career. If the steps are well-known then perhaps there is a different view of the problem or delegation that will better suit a creative member of the team.

### Share experiences, don't instruct

As the work progresses there's a chance that the manager will see a pattern or similar situation arise. There's a good chance the way that experience is communicated can come across as either 'sage sharing of experiences' or 'more micromanaging'. If there are experiences to share, then share the story and allow the learning to take place by allegory and not turn the learning into 'just do these steps'.

### Listen to progress, don't review it

Just as managers should be delegating the problem, not the steps to solving it, when it comes to a time for progress to be reported it is best to let folks report on the progress the way it works best. Micromanaging can also take the form of being specific about how progress should be reported or 'summoning' people to review the progress. If folks have been asked to take on a project, make sure they have the freedom to define the mechanics of the project as well.

### Provide feedback, don't course correct

Things might not always be going as well as everyone wants and when that happens managers can sometimes slip into 'gotta get this fixed' mode. This type of course correction can remove many of the downstream benefits of delegation and turn into a big negative for folks. It not only disempowers, but demotivates. When things aren't going well, the time is right for honest feedback and a two-way dialogue.

Communicate in the right way and at the right time, don't slow progress

All projects have more work and less time than they need. One way to reduce the amount of time available to make forward progress is for management to call for reviews or updates in a formal manner (meetings, written reports). This type of communication can slow things down – the preparation, the review, the general stand-down while these work products are created. Find the balance between contacting the team too little and bugging them too much.

Above all, treat people as you would like to be treated

If you are the type of person that is eager to request and receive feedback then chances are you won't see an eager manager as micromanaging you. But if you are the type of person who likes some elbow room and your manager is the eager provider of feedback, then that mismatch is likely to be perceived as micromanagement rather than empowering delegation.

### ...and be prepared to do it all virtually

Starting a new role may require connecting with people virtually. If so:

- Pay attention to how you come across (clothes, appearance, background, the language you use).

- Take time to get to know the people you are connecting with.

- Pace yourself – ideally, every 60 minutes speaking online should be followed by 30 minutes of reflection. Avoid the mistake of back-to-back virtual meetings, which can be exhausting and, as a result, undermining for someone looking to get established in a new role.

- Provide energy, thoughtfulness and empathy – check in with people and make sure all is well with them.

## Succeeding in your new role

- What information do you need before starting your new role? How can you acquire this information quickly?

- What are likely to be the most significant working relationships? Can you start building these before you take up your new role?

- How much time do you plan to set aside for yourself and your family? If you are moving location, what will you do to get to know your new environment?

- What expectations do you have – what do you want to achieve – and what are your boss's expectations? Are these reasonable? Can you manage expectations so that you achieve what is possible, while allowing yourself to excel and to exceed expectations?

- Are you aware of your leadership and decision-making style? Do you know how your behaviour affects others, and do you have the right style, mindset and attitude?

- Have you set time aside to understand the issues and plan your approach to the new role? Are you leaving your current role in a professional and supportive way, giving your successor the same support that you will need in your new role?

- Do you have a balanced and clear perspective about the business – its strengths and weaknesses, products, markets, customers, people and opportunities?

- Are you ready to engage people in your new role? Are you prepared to build coalitions with others? This is essential, if you are to identify and achieve early wins.

- What long-term changes might be needed? Do you have a broad timescale for what you would like to achieve, and the actions needed to accomplish this?

- Are you ready to develop a vision for the business – a view of the future to guide people's actions, to challenge and inspire individuals and to appeal to customers and other stakeholders?

- Have you assessed your own weaknesses? Is there a mentor or coach you could work with to support you during the transition and to help you achieve your aims?

## Planning and prioritizing your transition to the new role

- What do you need to learn most urgently, and how can you accelerate your learning?

- Who are the individuals critical to your success, and how can you build credibility with them?

- How should you pursue alignment between your team and the strategy, structure, systems, skills and culture of the organization?

- What are your personal shortcomings during transitions, and how can you compensate for these?

## Avoiding the pitfalls and challenges of a new role

- Where are you likely to make mistakes? Where are you vulnerable?

To assess your vulnerability, complete the following exercise. Rate yourself on a scale from 1 (not vulnerable) to 5 (you are very vulnerable). Also, ask a boss and a close colleague who know you well and whose opinion you respect to rate your susceptibility.

| Trap | Your susceptibility to the pitfalls of being a new boss, in the view of: | | |
|---|---|---|---|
| | Yourself | Your boss | A colleague |
| Failing to prepare in sufficient depth | | | |
| Isolation – emphasizing data over relationships | | | |
| Arriving with all the answers | | | |
| Keeping an existing team for too long | | | |
| Going too far too fast | | | |
| Being too closely associated with the wrong people | | | |
| Allowing unrealistic expectations and failing to agree objectives | | | |

### Assessing your credibility

- The following elements can help build personal credibility. How do you rate yourself on a scale from 1 (low effectiveness) to 5 (highly effective)?

- How would a boss and a close colleague rate you?

| Credibility element | Your effectiveness as a leader, viewed by: | | |
| --- | --- | --- | --- |
| | Yourself | Your boss | A colleague |
| Demanding but able to be satisfied | | | |
| Focused but flexible | | | |
| Active without causing commotion | | | |
| Willing to make tough calls but sensitive to the impact on others | | | |

- What implications are there for you on taking up your new job? Where are you most vulnerable – what can you do to minimize or eliminate this vulnerability?

- What should you do to avoid *vicious circles*?

- How can you benefit from *virtuous cycles*?

## Assessing the new business

Orientation questions can help you understand the business.

- What situation best describes the challenges and opportunities faced by the business? Is this situation clearly and widely recognized?

- What specific challenges are you likely to encounter? How can these be addressed?

- What are the major opportunities and what action is needed to realise them? Are there quick wins or 'low hanging fruit' that you can secure?

- What are the greatest risks, threats and potential pitfalls? How will these be avoided or overcome?

- What are the expectations of key stakeholders? Are these expectations realistic – do they need adjusting?

- What are your priorities?

## Questions to ask before starting in a new role

Initially it can be valuable to develop working hypotheses about the major strategic, technical and political challenges facing the organization.

- How do your strengths and shortcomings match the organization's challenges and the requirements of the new role? What issues or situations do you need to pay particular attention to?

- What signals will you give people from the start?

- Who will you speak with so as to gain the simplest, most accurate view of strategy and capabilities?

- Is the strategy robust and effective – now and in the future? Where is it taking us and what gaps are evident?

- What do outside experts see as the strategy's strengths and weaknesses?

- What do financial indicators and other performance measures indicate about the business's real priorities?

- What do outside observers (such as customers and analysts) think about how the organization is managed? How positive is their view and why?

- What do performance indicators and management reports reveal about how the organization really runs?

- Is the organization collaborative – do decision-making processes work well across functional boundaries?

## Questions to consider within the first few weeks

Within the first few weeks it is valuable to identify where to find out detailed information, and begin to test hypotheses about how the organization actually works.

- What are your initial impressions of the organization – its atmosphere, levels of motivation, culture and approach? For example, is it energetic and busy or slow and sleepy?

- What do senior managers believe to be the main short-term problems and opportunities?

- What do senior managers view as the longer-term strategic priorities? How robust is their reasoning?

- What is the growth potential for the business and also the likely barriers to growth?

- Is there a consensus about these issues? If not, who is right?

- Are people clear and honest about the problems they face (including their own shortcomings, as well organizational factors)?

- How much co-operation or conflict is there among key groups?

- Do people's attitudes and approaches match the urgency of the situation?

- Do employees understand the direction their business is heading and know what will ensure success?

## Questions to develop your learning in a sustained way, after the first few weeks

Once you are settled into the new role it is time to generate working hypotheses about the capabilities of colleagues, assess how well the organization interacts with customers, and form a view on what the organization does well and where it needs to improve.

- Who holds power and influence in the organization?

- Where are the main growth opportunities? Is there 'low-hanging fruit' that can be gained quickly?

- What are the greatest current challenges and potential threats?

- Are the right people in the right positions?

- Are people focused on meeting customer needs?

- Are people reliable? Do employees deliver what they promise and worry when deadlines are missed?

- Who seems to defer to whom? Who has the power and influence, and why?

- Are the necessary resources, operations, sales and service capabilities in place to deliver what customers need?

- Have you heard people praise or criticize the organization's level of skills and knowledge, processes, structure or strategy? How accurate and significant is their view?

- Do planned products look promising? How will they be better than competitors; why will customers buy?

## Questions to ask a new colleague or project team when collaborating for the first time

- What is the vision, the desired outcome, and what are our goals for this project?

- How will we achieve these goals, what process will we use and how will we work together as a team?

- What is the plan: who will do what, and by when?

- What are the key milestones?

- What resources do we need?

- Who are the key stakeholders and how will we keep them involved and informed?

- What are our individual working styles, our strengths, and weaknesses?

- What do we need from each other to do our best work?

- How often (and when) will we give each other feedback?

- How will we support each other and ensure we learn and improve?

## Questions to help you sustain momentum and progress during your first year

- Whose support do you need to gain to ensure that your changes succeed? Whose support can you count on?

- What are your top priorities?

- Who has to be replaced and how will this be done?

- Can productivity be improved – if so, how?

- What must happen to improve the effectiveness and timeliness of important decisions?

- Who is well motivated and who isn't? How significant is the issue of motivation?

- What are you doing well, what do you want to do better – and how will you do this?

So, question, listen, build relationships, be self-aware and set clear goals for yourself and, if appropriate, for others too. That will get you well on the way in a new leadership role.

# CHAPTER 14

# After Action Reviews and Feedback Questions

An after action review (commonly known as an AAR) is a structured assessment of the lessons from a situation or 'action' – for example what went well, what could have been done better, and what insights we need to carry forward. The value of an AAR is its ability to achieve several valuable results. First, it focuses on why things happened, increasing understanding. It also enables you to compare intended results with what was actually accomplished; it encourages participation, and it emphasizes trust and the value of feedback. AARs are a vital, valuable opportunity to initiate a coaching discussion: they provide content and context, and their immediacy and obvious relevance can result in a significant lasting change.

## Understand the benefits of AARs and prioritize them

For an AAR to be successful, the team needs to discover for itself the lessons provided by the experience. The more open and honest the discussion, the better. The key elements of an effective AAR are outlined below. Help your coachee to understand each of these elements:

### Discuss the purpose and rules

- The AAR does not seek to criticize negatively, or find fault. The emphasis should be on learning, so make this clear right from the start to achieve maximum involvement, openness and honesty.

**Encourage active participation**

- When setting the rules, the coachee needs to build trust. Emphasize that it's OK to disagree and that blame isn't part of the discussion. Personal attacks must be stopped immediately. Setting the right tone for an AAR is extremely important.

**Discuss team performance**

- The AAR is not about individual performance. Encourage your coachee to look at how the team performed, and don't assign blame.

**Conduct the AAR as soon as possible**

- For feedback to be effective, it should be timely. By doing an AAR quickly, the coachee will get a more accurate description of what happened. It also helps ensure that all (or most) of the team can participate.

**Focus the discussion with skilful questioning**

- If the coachee asks, 'How do you think that went?' this can be too broad a topic to discuss. Instead, they are better served by directing participants to think about specific issues or areas: 'How well did you cooperate?' 'How could communication have been better?' 'What planning activities were most effective?'

Discussion typically centres around three themes:

1. What was supposed to happen? What did happen? Why was there a difference?

2. What worked? What didn't work? Why?

3. What would you do differently next time?

It helps to start by getting participants to agree on what was supposed to happen. If the original objectives were unclear, then it's unlikely that the project or activity was very successful. Once you have an agreement, you can discuss actual versus intended results. You may need to return to the objectives as you move on to what worked and what you would do differently.

Useful questions to ask the person who you are coaching include:

- What would you have preferred to happen?

- What would you do differently next time?

- How could the situation have been prevented?

- In your opinion, what is the ideal procedure?

Sometimes it's helpful to have participants each write down their ideas, and then ask everyone to share. This helps you avoid group-think, and it allows quieter individuals to contribute.

## Encourage the coachee to let the team talk and record their recommendations

This is an exercise in good communication, not just feedback and continuous learning. The better the team members communicate with one another and work out differences, the stronger they'll be in the future – as both individuals and team players.

Ask your coachee to write down the specific recommendations made by the team. Then forward this information to other team leaders and stakeholders. This is how AARs contribute to organization-wide learning and improvement.

## Follow-up and provide support

If no one follows up on the recommendations, then time spent on the process is wasted. Create a system to ensure that the ideas gathered in the AAR are incorporated into operations and training activities.

## Gathering feedback from different perspectives – the five views

To help structure feedback it can help to consider a situation from five perspectives:

1. the outsider's view

2. The insider's view

3. the view from the bottom

4. the view from the top

5. the lateral view – from the middle.

When adopting different perspectives ask your coachee to consider the following questions:

- How does each group perceive your organization and its dealings with key external constituencies?

- What are seen as the organization's strengths and weaknesses?

- What problems do people mention? Are people's impressions consistent? If not, what do you think accounts for the discrepancy?

### The outsider's view

This is gained by consulting with customers, suppliers, distributors and others who interact with you, your organization or team. Talk to knowledgeable representatives of these key external groups; also, speak with strategic allies, analysts and local community and government leaders. If you are heading up a unit within a larger entity, it may be appropriate to consult internal suppliers and customers.

- What is our reputation or brand?

- How would you describe us (what three adjectives would you choose)? Specifically, how would you describe our character or approach?

- What are we known for?

- What do we do well?

- What could we improve or do better?

- What could we do more often?

- What aspect of our style or approach could be improved?

- How do we make you feel?

- How would you prefer us to make you feel?

- If you were us/me, what would you change or do differently?

- Can you provide examples of what we do/did well?

- From your point of view, how could we improve?

## The insider's view

This results from looking from the inside out. Consult experts on the front line who deal regularly with customers, suppliers, distributors and other external stakeholders. In particular, consult representatives of sales staff, new product or service developers, purchasing, logistics and distribution, quality assurance, corporate affairs and investor relations. This enables you to understand your situation from both sides.

- What needs to change?

- Who needs to change – and in what ways?

- How are our principles – the things guiding our work, and could these be improved?

- Do you know what makes us different and special?

- From your point of view, how could we improve?

## The view from the bottom

To understand the view from the bottom, talk to first line managers and employees in key functions. This will tell you how people further down in the organizational hierarchy perceive actions higher up. Consult representatives of production and service workers, and their supervisors, research and development, marketing, finance, information technology and management.

- How do you think things are going?

- What information do you need – what would help?

- What additional resources or support would be useful?

- What would improve your situation?

- What problems do people report that others in the organization do not?

- From your point of view, how could we improve?

## The view from the top

This is gained by consulting with senior managers in operations, research and development, marketing, finance, information technology and management.

- How does each group perceive your organization?

- What should we do more of or do better?

- What do we need to know or understand better, or prioritize more?

- What do you see as our strengths and weaknesses?

- What problems do you observe?

- Is there consistency between what top people tell you and what their direct reports say?

## The lateral view

The lateral view is gained by working with people who operate across business boundaries. They are well placed to look across the business from a central vantage point. People to consult with include product managers, project and programme managers, heads of task forces and project work groups, as well as informal liaisons between functional groups.

- How can we do more together?

- How can I/we help you?

- What insights or lessons have you learned?

- How do you view our performance: what do we do well, and what could we improve?

- Could you provide examples of times you have been impressed by our work – and times when you have not?

## Asking for personal feedback

Asking for personal feedback and displaying a desire to learn, develop and improve is a vital skill, and a sign of confidence and strength. Questions to ask your coachee include:

- Do you ask for feedback often enough?

- Do you seek feedback at the right time, in the right way (e.g. without defensiveness), and from the right people?

- What sort of feedback do you request?

- Why – and when – do you hesitate?

- Do you go 'deep' enough – for instance, asking for examples that illustrate the feedback?

- How does the feedback from others compare with your view of yourself?

- Do you ask for feedback that is specific (with examples) and actionable?

- Are you sufficiently warm, open and grateful – inviting reflective feedback?

- Do you consider feedback enough?

- Are you sufficiently open to changing? If not, why, and how can you change this?

- How well (how deeply) do you reflect on the feedback you have been given?

- Do you always follow the rules of feedback? Specifically: a) it is a gift, so treat it as such (and say 'thank you'!); b) don't be defensive; regardless of whether it is true someone, for some reason, thinks it is, and that alone makes it worth considering, and c) the best feedback results in a change, it acts as a catalyst, and that requires you to do something different.

# CHAPTER 15

# Future-Thinking Questions

Being future fit means preparing ourselves for the future, shifting our mindset, and thinking differently about how we operate as leaders. This can be accomplished by developing adaptive intelligence. This is a term from psychology that refers to the ability of the mind to be able to change in response to current demands in the environment.

Consider how effective you or your coachee is with each of the four characteristics of adaptive intelligence. Where could you improve, and how?

- The ability to live with uncertainty and change

- The ability to embrace change and unfamiliar circumstances as opportunities to understand, learn and improve

- The ability to embrace diversity

- The ability to nurture opportunity for self-organization.

## The ability to live with uncertainty and change

Knowing your personal threshold for change and disruption is important, because it shows you the moments when you'll need to reach out for help or guidance.

In addition, our mindset and thinking about the future needs to include strategies for dealing with unknown and disruptive forces in innovative ways. It particularly requires openness, a constructive approach, and resilience. Remember this useful insight from management guru Peter Drucker's *The Practice of Management*: 'The greatest danger in times of turbulence is not turbulence itself, but to act with yesterday's logic.'

With this in mind, ask yourself or your coachee:

- How effective are you in times of uncertainty and change?

- What can you do to be more open, enquiring and resilient?

- What do you need to learn?

- What mindset shifts, new beliefs and insights would help you embrace uncertainty and change?

- What practical issues do you need to address to be better able to cope with change?

### The ability to embrace change and unfamiliar circumstances as opportunities to understand, learn and improve

Learning is a key characteristic of what it means to be adaptable and remain on track to achieve objectives. Peter Senge's concept of the 'learning organization' captures what this ability can mean for an individual and a business: '...organizations where people continually expand their capacity to create the results they truly desire, where new and expansive patterns of thinking are nurtured, where collective aspiration is set free, and where people are continually learning to see the whole together' (*The Fifth Discipline*).

In a future characterized by change and disruption, embracing a holistic culture of learning and continuous improvement could mean the difference between success and catastrophic failure.

Ask yourself or your coachee:

- What do you need to understand better?

- When are the key moments to run a feedback or review session?

- How do you think, act and respond in times of: volatility, confusion, complexity, and ambiguity? Are there common recurring issues that you can address?

- Is there a disconnect between how you intend to act and how you actually act?

- Is there a disconnect between how you think you are acting, and what others experience?

## The ability to embrace diversity

Diversity of talent, experience and ideas brings commercial benefits, it can open up new ways of thinking, inspire innovation and leverage deep-seated knowledge to be applied in new and exciting ways.

Ask yourself or your coachee:

- How diverse is your thinking?

- How inclusive of different perspectives is your team?

- Do you share the belief that one of the defining elements of a future-oriented leader is the ability to incorporate a diverse team and support network – if so, what are you doing about this?

- Who can help you realize ambitious goals and overcome the challenges you encounter?

- Do you possess the mindset and focus to genuinely embrace diversity and unlock the free thinking, creative talent of tomorrow?

- What more can you do to encourage and ensure greater diversity of thinking and experience?

## The ability to nurture opportunity for self-organization

Adaptive intelligence means being able to relinquish control in order to build creative and self-sustaining teams.
Ask yourself or your coachee:

- Does your leadership and communication style do enough to build teams with trust and accountability as core values?

- Do you accept that many challenges require ever greater collaboration, agility and innovative thinking – if so, what are you doing to promote these qualities? What more can you do?

- How could your team work better?

- How can you increase trust and understanding between colleagues?

## Focusing on the future for you, your team and organization: visualization and future orientation

Visualization means enabling coachees to develop a coherent description of how their plans will develop in the future. A clear, dynamic vision provides a clear focus for action, guiding people's decisions at all levels and helping to instil confidence and resolve.

An essential element of visualization is future orientation – the ability to communicate a clear view of the future of a business:

its aims and what it's achieving. Future orientation applies to managers at all levels, whereas visionary thinking is most relevant to senior and mid-level managers. Useful questions to help with visualization for yourself or your coachee include:

- Do you regularly use visualization techniques at a personal level?

- Do you use visualization to enable someone to get a clear focus on a development or behavioural change goal?

- Are you doing enough as a leader to set the right course and then take people with you?

- Do you have a clear and dynamic vision of the future?

- Does your vision inspire, mobilize and engage people, unlocking energy and commitment? If not, what more can you do to achieve this?

- Does your vision provide a clear focus for the future, guiding actions and decisions at all levels? If not, what more can you do to achieve this?

- Does your vision promote confidence, determination and effectiveness? If not, what more can you do to achieve this?

- Do you trust your intuition enough? If you feel that a situation is changing and different, or if you've an idea that makes sense to you, explore it further.

- Do you test your assumptions? Insights don't readily come from old information, so look for trends and try to understand why things are changing, not just how.

- Do you offer colleagues a progressive view of the future – one that is imaginable, exciting and inspiring, communicable, desirable and realistic, focused and adaptive? The vision needs to be general enough to accommodate individual initiatives, and flexible enough to allow for changing conditions.

- How is the situation likely to alter over time?

- Are the people involved prepared (in terms of attitude) and skilled (in terms of ability) to react to changing situations? How can this be measured? What remedial action might be needed?

- What is likely to prevent you and your colleagues from fulfilling your vision?

- How will you and your colleagues pre-empt these challenges, or react to any unforeseen problems?

---

### Questioning: the indispensable skill for coaches and leaders

Questioning is an essential part of coaching: an indispensable skill that enables us to learn, develop our thinking, and arrive at an answer, insight or course of action. For a coach, great questions guide without being directive, they explore and explain without teaching or preaching, they gently encourage, support and challenge without taking over. They allow coaches to influence, develop and shape someone's thinking far beyond that of their own knowledge or area of expertise, propelling the learner to new levels of insight, awareness, action and effectiveness.

I hope these questions stimulate, sustain and guide you and the people around you in times of opportunity, challenge and progress.

---

# Notes on Sources and Further Reading

Bibb, Sally, (2017) *The Strengths Book: Discover How to be Fulfilled in Your Work and in Life*, LID

Charan, Ram, Stephen Drotter & James Noel, (2011) *The Leadership Pipeline*, 2nd edn, Jossey-Bass

Cowen, Alan S. & Dacher Keltner, (19 September 2017) 'Self-report Captures 27 Distinct Categories of Emotion Bridged by Continuous Gradients', *PNAS* 114.38: E7900–E7909.

Drucker, Peter F., (2006) *The Practice of Management*, reissue edn, HarperBusiness

Dweck, Carol S., (2017) *Mindset: Changing The Way You Think to Fulfil Your Potential*, updated edition, Robinson

Goleman, Daniel, (2020) *Emotional Intelligence: Why It Can Matter More than IQ*, Twenty-fifth Anniversary Edition, Bloomsbury

Hall, Edward T., (1988) *The Hidden Dimension*, Bantam Doubleday Dell

Hammond, John S., Ralph L. Keeney & Howard Raiffa, (September–October 1998) 'The Hidden Traps in Decision Making', *Harvard Business Review 76/5*: 47–8, 50, 52

Hofstede, Geert, Gert Jan Hofstede & Michael Minkov, (2010) *Cultures and Organizations: Software of the Mind: Intercultural Cooperation and Its Importance for Survival* 3rd edn, McGraw-Hill Education

Kotter, John, (2012) *Leading Change*, Harvard Business Review

Senge, Peter M., (2006) *The Fifth Discipline: The Art and Practice of the Learning Organization*, 2nd edn, Random House Business

Thomas–Kilmann Conflict Mode, https://kilmanndiagnostics.com/overview-thomas-kilmann-conflict-mode-instrument-tki/

Trompenaars, Fons, Interview with author 2010

Trompenaars, Fons & Charles Hampden-Turner, (2020) *Riding the Waves of Culture: Understanding Diversity in Global Business*, Nicholas Brealey

Tuckman, Bruce W., (1965) 'Developmental Sequence in Small Groups', *Psychological Bulletin* 63.6: 384–99

# Acknowledgements

This book is inspired by many people. First, sincere thanks and gratitude are due to Holly Bennion, publisher at Hachette, who firmly believed in the value of a book of coaching questions and then had the confidence to suggest that I might be the one to write it. Holly and her colleagues at Hachette are exceptional and their warm, engaging professionalism, creativity and support are all immensely valued.

I also owe a huge debt to all my clients, coachees and colleagues over the years who have, without doubt, provided the most exciting and stimulating environment in which to work, learn and develop.

Towards the end of the writing process I posed a question on LinkedIn asking for great coaching questions. The response was hugely encouraging: over 5,000 views and a wide range of questions, comments and insights. Thanks are certainly due to those coaches who took the time to respond: your encouragement and insightfulness is appreciated. I am particularly grateful to: Maria Katsarou-Makin, Lydia Kan, Jonathan Besser, Marieluise Maiwald, Seema Arora, Claudia Deniers, Eric Poll, Antonija Pacek, Saira Chaudry, Adrian Kirk, Penny de Valk, and Alison Beck.

One important meta-level point was made online: as a coach and leader, questioning is a mindset as well as being something you do, and questioning is the flipside of listening. Questions are not a panacea on their own. Questioning, listening and positive intent are essential and mutually supportive: they all rely on each other.

In this book I have tried to provide relevant guidance and context to support coaches and leaders, so that the most effective questions are being asked with the right mindset, in the right way and at the right time, with relevant tools, models and insights also at hand to help.

It seems to be an inescapable fact of our time – an irony, perhaps – that the more we know, the more questions we have, and the more we achieve, the greater our need for support. What is clear is that we need leaders now as much as we ever have; effective leadership starts and grows within us, and leadership is encouraged and developed with coaching.

And great questions, asked thoughtfully and with positive intent, lie at the heart both of coaching and leadership.

I hope these ideas and questions will provide you with the inspiration to find out more, stimulating your thinking as a coach and leader along new, creative lines, and helping you develop your own effectiveness and coaching style.

*Jeremy Kourdi*